T. Margaret Sandige —

DON'T LET THE FUNNY STUFF GET AWAY

Keep 'Em Laughing —

Jeanne Robertson

2009

Other books *Coauthored* and Authored
by Jeanne Robertson

How the Platform Professionals Keep 'Em Laughin'
Humor: The Magic of Genie
Mayberry Humor Across the USA

DON'T LET THE FUNNY STUFF GET AWAY

Turn Everyday Experiences into Stories that Audiences Will Remember!

Jeanne Swanner Robertson

Rich Publishing Company
10611 Creektree • Houston, Texas

To
Carolyn Ellis Lipscomb,
Storyteller Extraordinaire

First Edition 1998
First Printing, August 1998

Library of Congress Catalog Card No. 98-67045
ISBN 0-927577-03-8

Printed in the United States of America.
98 99 00 01 02 03 – 7 6 5 4 3 2 1

TABLE OF CONTENTS

FOREWORD

Back in 1980, I wrote a book called "Public Speaking for Private People" in which I covered the problems of the average person when it comes to telling jokes: "The best advice I can give you as you're trying to launch yourself as a public speaker is this: Don't tell jokes! Humor is the riskiest, least understood, and highest paid of the performing arts because humor requires timing, inflection, authority, and native skill that most people don't possess."

Everyone of us has suffered through meetings where inexperienced speakers lay a big, smelly egg right at the outset of their presentation when they tell a good joke badly, or pick the wrong joke to tell.

The reason people insist on attempting to be humorous when they have no skills in this art, is that a good laugh is so rewarding to both the audience and the speaker when it's done right.

Jeanne has provided in this book some priceless information: Keep it personal, make it brief, and tell it from your own life observation or experience. Even so, you will be on dangerous ground because humor is like blowing up a fragile bubble. . . its iridescence can be shattered if you blow it up too big or take too long to do it.

When you're telling about an embarrassing or surprising event, the point of the "joke" is generally yourself. . . which gives it authority, a genuine believable feeling, and will not insult anybody in your audience.

I rarely tell a funny story that involves religion until I mention that I am a Baptist preacher's son, and the story involves Baptists! Politics, baldness, overweight, and indelicate subjects are all land mines, waiting to explode in the speaker's face.

There are two types of "joke insurance" that I frequently use even though I've spent a lifetime fine-tuning my own story-telling skills. The first type might be called "famous authority insurance" because it involves attributing your story to some well known humorist.

You might say, "Bob Hope used to tell a great joke about his first time in the White House". . . or "Jerry Seinfeld always says that his funniest programs are about nothing. . . well. . . I have a story about nothing that resulted in my getting married. . ." In this way, you authenticate the humor by leaning on the famous name you use in introducing your own story.

The second kind of humor insurance might be called the "meaningful point" type. The idea here is to tell the funny story *not* just to get a laugh but also to make a point that furthers the main subject of your speech.

And, finally, I'm sure that Jeanne agrees with me that the longer your "funny" story takes to tell, the stronger finish you have to make. If you take five minutes to tell a story, you're asking your audience to invest a lot of time and attention and therefore it expects to get back more in the end. Remember. . . the main thing you're trying to do with your anecdotes is paint an illustrative picture to explain your concept to your audience.

Your primary purpose in being there is not to get people to laugh.

Sooo. . . "Don't Let the Funny Stuff Get Away" and start your own "Rolodex" of personal anecdotes the minute you put down this funny, interesting, and practical book my friend has written.

—Art Linkletter

ACKNOWLEDGMENTS

My sincere appreciation to all of the individuals who assisted in this project, and especially to the following:

The people who listened to my explanation of the LAWS for finding life-experience material and who tried variations of Jeanne's Journal System. Their suggestions were most valuable to the continuation of the project. Thank you to business executive *Tom Bass*, trainer and consultant *Bobbie Avant Brown*, professional speaker *Jim Folks*, Toastmaster and businessman *Ted Gorman*, minister *Rich Greenway*, aspiring writer *Ruth Lee*, writer and storyteller *Carolyn Lipscomb*, teacher *Margaret Parham*, collegiate tennis coach *Tom Parham*, college vice president *Nan Perkins*, professional speaker *Linda Pulliam*, businesswoman *Katherine Swanner*, professional woman and Toastmaster *Elizabeth Turner*, and college athletic director *Dr. Alan White*.

The several groups that permitted me to explain the Journal System to their members in preparation for this book. The feedback was sincere and most helpful. Thank you to the

New York Tri-State Chapter of the National Speakers Association, the *North Texas Speakers Association*, the *New England Speakers Association*, the *National Speakers Association Foundation*, and *District 37 of Toastmasters International*.

Humorist and author *Liz Curtis Higgs*, for her interest, direction and guidance. She epitomizes Thomas Jefferson's quote, "He who lights his taper at mine receives light without darkening me."

Toni Meredith, my friend and secretary of twenty years, for all she has done to assist with my humor journals. Toni is an excellent reminder of the power of a comment such as "Hey, this journal thing really works!"

Lan Lipscomb, Norma White, Patricia Fripp, and *Terri Lonier* for their contributions to the project.

Dennis Hill for a terrific jacket design.

Bob Bubnis with BookSetters for his creative ideas.

My editor, *Lila Empson*, who must have laughed at my many naive questions but who always treated me with the utmost respect. She could have been making any number of writers look good during the time she allocated for me. I appreciate her invaluable assistance.

Dobby Dobson at Rich Publishing Company for his continued faith in my ideas and his guidance in making them come true. Horror stories abound about authors and publishers, but through four publications I have found working with Dobby always to be a pleasure.

My longtime colleagues and humor buddies in Platform Professionals, *Doc Blakely, Robert Henry*, and *Al Walker*.

And finally, special thanks to my husband, *Jerry*, who continues to support my many projects.

INTRODUCTION

The purpose of this book is to communicate my system for gathering funny stories from everyday experiences. As a professional, humorous speaker since 1963, I have relied on funny, original stories from my life experiences rather than on jokes. Audiences like my approach, and I always have more speaking invitations than I can possibly accept.

In order to collect as much funny stuff as possible, I developed a method for collecting life-experience humor. This system—jokingly dubbed Jeanne's Journal System by my peers in the National Speakers Association—has worked extremely well for me. It has helped me find and record an abundance of unique stories, and can help you do the same. I am excited about sharing this information. Following the system will demand discipline and require a change in your approach to finding humor. It will also be fun.

Throughout my career I have received numerous phone calls and letters from both beginning and experienced speakers. The following letter represents a typical inquiry:

Jeanne,

I've been in Toastmasters International for several years–a most valuable experience for developing leadership and communication skills. To continue to improve and to learn more about the speaking business, I joined the National Speakers Association and attended the last convention. I was blown away. I am now even more excited than ever about speaking.

The top speakers in Toastmasters International and the National Speakers Association seem to have unending supplies of humorous stories that make their programs so satisfying. I have been unable to figure out where they get all these stories.

People in my NSA chapter said that you are known for using funny, original material and that you have a system for finding these stories.

Tell me, Jeanne. Where do you get your material? Help!

Hundreds of similar letters, telephone calls, and e-mails all ask essentially the same question: Where do I get my material? Where do I find the funny stuff, the stories and true vignettes that illustrate my points?

In this book I will share my system (I love to tell all about it!) for gathering humor from life experiences. You will learn how to:

- Take advantage of life-experience stories in your speaking or writing
- Use my LAWS to gather funny stories from your everyday experiences
- Understand Jeanne's Journal System

- Develop your personal system for gathering humorous, original stories

Who Will Benefit From This Book?

This book is for everyone who needs a large supply of humorous, real-life stories to use in speaking and writing:

- *Professional speakers*, specifically my colleagues in the National Speakers Association, who require a changing supply of personal stories
- *Toastmasters*, who constantly need new material for the same audience
- *Trainers and workshop leaders*, who spend hours upon hours before the same people
- *Ministers*, who must find new illustrations for weekly sermons
- *Writers*, who need an assortment of unique vignettes for articles, newsletters, and books
- *Educators*, who know the value of humor in the classroom
- *Athletic directors and coaches*, who are called upon to speak at clinics, conventions, and banquets

What This Book Is Not!

If you need a large supply of humorous life-experience stories, you will definitely benefit from this book. Will it answer all your questions on finding material for speaking and writing? Goodness no. Below are a few things this book is *not*.

- *Don't Let the Funny Stuff Get Away* is not a joke book. (Although humorous examples from my journals illustrate my points.)

- It is not a book on how to become a professional speaker. (But Jeanne's Journal System in Part III gives you the flavor of my profession.)
- It is not a book on journaling. (But you'll learn how to keep a humor journal that could become one of your new best friends.)
- It is not a book on how to make a speech or write a book. (But it provides a system that will supply stories to enhance both.)
- It does not provide intricate computer information for organizing material. I'm happy to share what I do on my word processor, but I'm a humorist, not a computer guru. I'm betting that each reader will be able to figure out how to use their computer effectively to meet his or her needs. (Whew. Got out of that.)
- It is not for people who need only a few stories. (It is for people who need a large supply of life-experience stories at their fingertips but don't have large amounts of time to spend looking for them or don't want to devote large amounts of time looking for them. Hear me now! If you don't need a whole truckload of stories, this is not for you. If you're planning one speech to be given one time at one special event, you do not need this information. If you have to write one article a year, this book will be a waste of your time.)
- Finally, and most important, you probably have sensed by now that *Don't Let the Funny Stuff Get Away* is not for a wide audience. (When my daddy wanted to really emphasize something, he'd start or end his sentence with "nosiree, bob." Since my name is Jeanne, that seemed curious to me, but that was his way of stressing something. So this book is not for everybody, nosiree, bob.)

My publisher and friends who know the ins and outs of marketing have told me repeatedly that *Don't Let the Funny Stuff Get Away* will have limited market appeal.

I know that. I'm looking for the few...the organized...the dedicated story seekers.

The Proof Is in the Using

Don't Let the Funny Stuff Get Away aids the user in gathering real-life stories either randomly (which is good enough for many people) or through a more detailed approach. I will use examples from Jeanne's Journal System using the LAWS I'll present and from stories that found their way into speeches.

"This-one-might-work material" will not be included. I have field-tested all of the illustrations in speeches across the country.

I have included a few repeat examples from my earlier books that are particularly good illustrations of how to gather material that you can pull out and use.

And to show how the system truly works, most of the stories are brand-new. Enjoy!

How This Book Is Organized

Don't Let the Funny Stuff Get Away contains four main sections. If you have a question that's unanswered at a particular point, keep plodding ahead. Odds are, I didn't realize that you are as smart as you are (!) and that you would be asking that question so early. Keep reading; I'll get around to your question in due time.

Here are brief descriptions of the four sections and what you'll find in each one.

Part I: The Advantages of Using Life-Experience Humor

In this section, I'll lay out my case for using humor from life experiences rather than material from joke books or stories that have been created by others. There is a lot of stuff in this section about me and how I got into professional speaking, and it explains why I believe so strongly in this type of humor.

If you already agree with me that life-experience humor is the best way to go, this section will be a breeze. No heavy thinking. Just a validation of what you know.

Part II: The LAWS of Finding Life-Experience Humor

You can read the whole book, draw up your humor journal and have the best intentions in the world, but you'll find yourself staring off into space if you don't obey the LAWS of finding life-experience stories that are outlined in Part II. Worse yet, you may become so discouraged that you may revert to old joke books or other speakers' cassettes for material. (Don't do it! Don't do it!) Part II explains the LAWS that are sure to help you. You'll become a trained noticer as you *look, listen,* and *ask* for humor. You'll learn when to *write up* and when to *stretch.*

This section is a re-reader. Any time your creativity hits low tide, read this section again. It's extremely important.

Part III: Jeanne's Journal System

Part III is where I present the system that has been effective for me for years. You will learn exactly how to set it up and how to work it. You don't have to use Jeanne's Journal System to gather humor. If you use only the LAWS in the last section, you will come out way ahead. But if you want to try the journal process, here it is. If you are a professional speaker who travels often or are an aspiring speaker, you should be able to take it and run with it.

I'll go through each category, tell you the rationale behind it, and illustrate the results with stories that came straight off this system.

Part IV: Developing Your Humor Journal

Don't travel? Don't speak professionally? Jeanne's Journal doesn't fit your needs? In this section, you'll learn how to develop a humor journal that does fit your needs. You will compile a journal step-by-step and learn what others found when they attempted to keep their humor journals.

If you're looking at a blank screen and pencil tapping by this point, this is the final information you need to get started.

Part I

THE ADVANTAGES OF USING LIFE-EXPERIENCE HUMOR

Chapter 1

THE ROAD THAT LED TO A SPEAKING CAREER

I was Miss North Carolina so far back that many of the events of my reign barely register now. I remember smiling a lot and perching on convertibles. But while I don't remember all of the little things connected with that time, the part that directed me into professional speaking stands out vividly in my memory.

When I won the title, I dropped out of Auburn University for a year, appeared at scores of North Carolina festivals and pageants, and ate my way through hundreds of luncheons and banquets. I never met a chicken I didn't recognize, no matter how it was disguised.

At each event I was expected to say a few words. Although I was only nineteen years old, it did not take me long to figure out that audiences liked it when I tried to be funny. Once they laughed, I was hooked.

At the beginning of the year, I told pat, clean jokes out of books. My pride tells me they were really funny, but now I realize they were well worn by the time I got them. I perfected

3

about seven of those jewels, and I told them well because I told them so often, sometimes two or three times a day.

I haven't repeated any of those jokes in years, but I believe that even now I could bolt straight up in the middle of the night and deliver them verbatim if I had to.

As that year progressed, I also begin telling the amusing incidents that naturally occurred for a six-foot-two basketball player with a crown on her head.

I began to sense that even though I got a great response with the jokes, I got an even more positive response when I told true stories. A couple of these were about such situations as drinking from my finger bowl at a formal banquet in Greensboro and being shot by kids with peashooters during a parade in Mount Olive. When I realized that those stories drew the most comments, I worked even harder to find more of them.

Word spread quickly through the state that Miss North Carolina could do more than cut ribbons and wave. She could also do fifteen minutes of funny stuff, but you might have trouble getting her off the stage.

In the middle of that year, the state Jaycees gave me two opportunities that further pushed me to look for material from my everyday experiences. A banquet for the eighty-four contestants, chaperons, judges, and numerous dignitaries would kick off the weeklong annual state pageant where I was to crown my successor.

Traditionally, the banquet was a staid, formal affair where they served something like Cornish hens. Surprisingly, however, the Jaycees asked me to be the after-dinner speaker. They wanted me to do what I had been doing since I had been crowned. They wanted me to be funny. "Just tell the stuff that happened all year," they kept emphasizing.

Knowing months in advance that I would be speaking thirty minutes that night heightened my resolve to find material. It was a great opportunity and I knew it. So was the second opportunity the Jaycees gave me.

North Carolina had the largest state pageant in the nation in those days. It was a four-night event with three evenings of preliminary competition and a big final night on statewide television.

This was precomputer, so toward the end of each evening of competition, there would be a lull while all the points were being tabulated. The judges often left the hall while everyone waited and waited for the results. Musical acts were typically inserted during the balloting, but my year, the state Jaycees asked me to fill that slot each night.

My instructions were to walk out on the stage and be funny until the scores were tabulated. No singers. No dancers. Just Jeanne telling her stories. Nobody knew in advance how long I would be out there. Fifteen minutes each night? Twenty-five? I was to keep talking until somebody gave me the signal to stop. I was thrilled.

My well-worn jokes were out. Everyone in the pageant community had heard them, and I certainly couldn't tell identical jokes four nights in a row. I spent the last months of my year working new vignettes into my daily acts. When a story clicked, I would put it aside for pageant week and work on something else.

That one week of filling with life-experience humor every night, plus the thirty-minute after-dinner speech, pushed me from being a pageant winner to a young speaker, and it gave me enough material to begin a professional career.

I crowned my successor and turned over the keys to the slick convertible. Three days later, I pulled out of my hometown of Graham in my daddy's 1954 Valiant and headed for

Wrightsville Beach to make my first speech crownless. It was for the North Carolina Alcohol Beverage Control Boards. I put my jokes on the back burner because the true stories had gone over so well the week before.

I certainly used jokes as my speaking career evolved, especially in the early days. And I occasionally use them now, as I will explain later. But my stock in trade has always been to tell true stories, admittedly sometimes slightly embellished. Today, 95 percent of my humorous material is based on my life experiences.

Chapter 2

WHY USE LIFE-EXPERIENCE HUMOR?

Why have I, as a professional speaker, continued to use life-experience humor? The simple answer is, *it works*. Audiences specifically mention the stories after my speeches, and meeting planners tell me that they book me because of my material. When those two groups talk, I listen.

Several years ago I keynoted the National Speakers Association annual convention. That opening slot called for me to be funny, of course, but also to introduce the theme, "The Art of Mastery."

In preparation, I studied over fifty individuals whom I deemed to be master speakers. They were the best in the business, the crème de la crème. I discovered that, without exception, master speakers are themselves on the platform and capitalize on what makes them different. Not a single one of them attempts to copy in any way the style, delivery, or material of another speaker. This means they have their own unique material, and the best place to find that is in their own lives.

Keep in mind that established professional speakers are in the business of...giving speeches. Like other entrepreneurs, the best ones know what it takes to be successful. Today's audiences and meeting planners are not excited by passed-around jokes, even really good jokes, because they've already heard them many times.

In recent years there has been a significant shift away from generic jokes, which were once the backbone of presentations, toward the use of personal stories. In short, successful professional speakers know and supply what today's audiences and meeting planners demand.

Life-experience humor offers a number of advantages. Life-experience humor

- Gives the speaker an identity.
- Lessens significantly the chances that the audience has heard the material.
- Allows the speaker to describe events with firsthand knowledge.
- Assures a never-ending supply of stories.
- Makes life more fun.
- Is easy to find.

Life-experience humor gives the speaker an identity. Audiences remember specific things about speakers who use humor from their life experiences rather than use routine jokes. These unique stories set speakers apart from the pack, and increase the chances that audiences will remember the messenger as well as the message. (We all want to be remembered!)

Life-experience humor lessens significantly the chances that the audience has heard the material. Successful speakers know that if they use standard jokes, they run the risk of using material not only already heard by the audience, but quite possibly heard earlier in that same meeting.

Today's audiences want their messages brought to them in an entertaining fashion, and they are an astute bunch. They live in a world of videos, CDs, cassettes, Internet joke services, and twenty-four-hour comedy channels. They hear top-notch comedians on a regular basis. They are joke savvy.

People who would never dream of giving a speech or writing an article quickly recognize much of the old material that has sustained speakers for years. They've not only heard much of this material, they have used it in conversations.

Unless you are one of the best joke tellers the group will ever have heard (an unlikely possibility for most of us) or unless you can guarantee that your audiences or readers have not heard your joke, you must search your personal experiences for fresh material.

Life-experience humor allows the speaker to describe events with firsthand knowledge. Stories take on new meaning and are more interesting when told in the first person. Stories are natural, appropriate, and tailored to the speaker. In addition, personal stories are easy to recall which cuts down the need for notes.

An athletic director, for instance, may gather stories from what's happening around him every day. Those sports-related stories work perfectly when he speaks at athletic banquets or alumni gatherings. They also serve him well when he speaks at the Rotary Club because, after all, he is an athletic director speaking from his world.

A financial manager may gather stories from small meetings with clients. Those stories add life to her next seminar on financial planning, and they tie into the reason people are there.

A trainer may gather stories during a five-day training session and include them in her next session with a new group. The material is relevant. It's comfortable. It fits the user and the situation.

Life-experience humor assures a never-ending supply of stories. Every day is filled with humor-gathering opportunities. Every situation is a possible story ready to be tapped. We can draw from our families, friends, and coworkers as well as from acquaintances and perfect strangers. Why use old jokes or create material from scratch when life writes it for us?

Life-experience humor makes life more fun. When speakers and writers decide to use stories from their everyday experiences, they begin to look at the world through humorous eyes. Doing so makes life more interesting. More fun.

After speaking part-time for thirteen years, I stopped teaching and coaching to pursue a full-time speaking career. Life-experience humor had always been a part of my material, but when I started traveling more frequently, I made an even more diligent effort to find and record the stories happening around me. Many speakers were relying solely on jokes at that time, and I believed I could get ahead of the game by going in the other direction.

During one trip, bad weather grounded all flights out of Atlanta and passengers were going nuts blaming gate agents and complaining loudly to whomever might listen. I took my tablet and pen and started lurking around grumpy people just to pick up funny lines that might become a piece of material.

After a while, I noticed that everyone was upset except me. I was so intent on finding the humor in the situation, admittedly for use as speech material, that I was keeping my own sense of humor. I was actually having a good time.

Since that time I've been highly cognizant that I could control my own disposition and attitude by looking for the humor in everyday situations, especially those that are stressful.

I also like to watch others do the same thing.

On another occasion, my plane had been sitting on the ground for almost thirty minutes past scheduled departure, and passengers were getting antsy. Suddenly the pilot clicked on intercom and announced, "Ladies and gentleman, I'm sorry for the delay. The machine that rips the handles off your bags is broken, and we're having to do it by hand."

Laughter erupted throughout the cabin and I watched people relax. My point exactly. Looking for humor from our everyday experiences makes life more fun.

Life-experience humor is easy to find. All you have to do to find life-experience humor is obey the LAWS that will be covered in the next section.

Chapter 3

THE BIG BAG PLAN

Oh, you *did* hear the one about...?

Wait! Wait! Does that mean jokes are out?

Absolutely not! A good joke that is told well and illustrates a specific point is a work of art.

This leads me to explain my Big Bag plan. Think of gathering humorous stories for speaking or writing as if filling up a Big Bag with good material that fits your style and purpose. You can draw from this Big Bag at any time. The more good material you store in your Big Bag, the more choices you give yourself. The goal is to have a large supply from which to select.

Life-experience humor is my mainstay, but every speaker's Big Bag should contain special jokes scattered amongst the life-experience stuff. The secret is in knowing what each one illustrates and when to pull it out. I maintain a small supply of jokes because I know that even an old joke will be a winner when told at the correct time and correct place. A speech I made in Nevada illustrates my point.

I was listed as the keynote speaker for a convention in Reno and was scheduled to speak from 11:00 to 12:00 during the opening general session, which started at 10:00. From the pounding of the gavel on, there was trouble. Every person introduced "said a few words," and before long, the program was running way behind. Eleven o'clock came and went, and I smiled my little beauty-pageant smile and waited patiently as committee chair after committee chair gave reports and people slipped out. By the time I was introduced (at 12:15!) more than three-fourths of the audience was gone. Watching people leave (and wishing I could go with them), I also mentally sifted through my Big Bag and found one of the oldest jokes around. When I was finally introduced I opened with it. I'll give you the joke, and then tell you why it worked.

A man was waiting to be introduced to deliver the keynote address at a convention, but the emcee kept introducing everything and everybody else in the room. To make matters worse, almost everyone who was introduced strode to the microphone and delivered an impromptu minipresentation. Award recipients thanked, outgoing officers reminisced, foundation fund-raisers begged, and people in the audience slipped out—in droves. Finally, only three people were left in the room: the keynoter, the emcee, and one other man.

After his introduction, the guest of honor stepped toward the front of the stage and said to the one lone fellow sitting out there, "You don't know how much I appreciate your staying."

The guy said, "Could you hurry it up? I'm the next speaker on the program."

When I was introduced over an hour late to a handful of people, this old joke brought down what was left of the house. Why? For one thing, it's a good story. More important, however, it fit the situation and *the audience knew it wasn't part of my planned remarks*. The same joke, told to open a regular speech, would seem out of place. People would think the truth, "She really wanted to work that one in." When introduced over an hour late, the whole situation changed.

Old joke books can be valuable. Use them to jump-start your creativity. On days when you're working on material but find yourself off to a slow start, pull out an old joke book and start reading. Within pages, you might read a joke that reminds you of something that happened on a trip or in your youth. You'll be off and running again. This rarely fails.

For example, when our son Beaver was in junior high school, he and his friends wanted to wear only Izod shirts. If there was no little alligator sewn somewhere on the garment, that garment hung in the closet until it no longer fit. In addition, the Izod shirts had to be worn with Levi jeans. Period.

In that same phase, Beaver and his buddies were attending numerous basketball camps in the summer. Time and time again we mothers received the typical camp letter telling us to make sure to sew labels in the clothes our boys brought to camp. With all this information, however, it wasn't until I was reading an old joke book that I developed the following piece of material.

❂ ❂ ❂

Our son Beaver went to four basketball camps last summer. Before one camp, the coach had the nerve to write me a letter that instructed, "Mrs. Robertson, When you bring your son to our camp, please do not mark his name in his clothes with a black laundry marker. We prefer that you use sewn-in labels with his name."

Sewn-in labels? Sure. I thought it was a joke letter. When I realized it wasn't, I put it on the floor and kicked it. Then I wrote them back.

"My name is Jeanne Robertson. I will be at camp with my son on July 13. His name is Levi Izod."

This was a great piece of material that I used until Beaver grew up and the Levi/Izod craze dwindled. (Current generations would have to think to understand it.) Was my junior high school aged son really a fanatic about wearing Izod and Levi clothing? Yes. Did one of the camps send me a letter requesting that the camper's name be sewn into each item of clothing? Yes. But I didn't get the idea for the piece of material until I was reading an old joke book and came upon a joke with a similar theme. The teller said his name was in all his clothing. Fruit of the Loom.

Study old joke books to get your creative energy flowing.

More important, study old books for jokes that fit certain speaking situations. Drop this material in your Big Bag to pull out and use when you need it. A word of advice: When you use a tried-and-true generic joke, preface it by saying, "You may recall the old story about…" or "Sitting here today, I couldn't help but be reminded of…" Your audience will then know you realize it is an old standard.

Speakers certainly can and should tell jokes, but you should rely mainly on life-experience stories. The top speakers know the value of a good joke that illustrates a specific point or fits the occasion. But they also know that if a joke illustrates a certain point and is well received, the audience will appreciate even more a personal story that does the same thing.

Part II

THE LAWS OF FINDING LIFE-EXPERIENCE HUMOR

Chapter 4

OBEY THE LAWS

I am not big on acronyms. I declare I'm not. It's seldom a thrill for me when a speaker spells out a long word and starts going through it letter by letter. At the end of the first one, I glance at my watch, check the number of letters left, and calculate how long the whole thing is going to take.

Too many times I've sat in audiences and wished the speaker would skip a letter or two, just for the heck of it, or misspell a word to see if people were paying attention. It's a personal thing.

Acronyms have always seemed to be a less-than-creative way to write an article or give a speech, but they seem to work for some people. One speaker I know has memorized a character trait for every letter in the alphabet. He takes the company or association name and starts hammering out advice at the blink of eye.

"The *A* in American Society of Plumbing Educators stands for *attitude!*" The *C* in Chamber of Commerce stands for *challenge!*" "The *U* in the University of North Carolina at Chapel Hill stands for *unique.*" (Another reason for going to

Duke. Shorter word.) The man can do the entire alphabet before I can walk around my block. He's *Z* for *zealous*!

You get my point. I am not crazy about acronyms.

Then, lo and behold, after telling friends this for years, an acronym turns out to be perfect right here. (What are we if not *F* for *flexible*?)

Certain LAWS make it easy to find humor from our life experiences. That's the acronym—LAWS. At least it's just four letters. Ignore these laws and you could be left storyless. Stick to the LAWS and material will gush forth. Well, for sure it trickles steadily.

So what are the LAWS for finding life-experience humor to use in speeches and writing?

Look and listen

Ask

Write UP

Stretch it

(How clever can a person get?)

But Before You Start

To obey the LAWS of finding humor from your life experiences, first give thought to the type of stories you need. This does not mean you're locked for eternity to one type of material. Goodness no. Speaking styles and goals change. For right now, however, know what you're looking for before you head out.

Answering the questions below will help determine the type of humor that fits your style of speaking or writing. (You might discuss this with a colleague who understands your goals and has heard you speak. There have been speakers who thought they were really funny but weren't. A friend may help honestly critique your ability to use humor.) There are no correct or incorrect answers. By carefully thinking through your answers, however, you'll discover what is right for you.

1. What is your purpose when you speak or write? To entertain? To teach? To motivate? To inform? To question? Are you supposed to be hilarious or at least slightly funny?

2. Can your humorous material be only mildly amusing or must it be drop-dead funny? Do you want your audiences to burst out laughing, smile, or nod in agreement when you tell a story? (Mildly amusing anecdotes that bring smiles may be fine for a trainer in an all-day session, but they will end the career of a humorist. As a general rule, mildly amusing anecdotes go farther in print than when delivered before a live audience.)

3. Who will generally be in your audiences? Families? All men? All women? Teenagers? Elderly? Young people? Upper-level managers? Entry-level employees?

4. Will your audiences appreciate slightly risqué illustrations? (Look out, you're treading on thin ice here.)

5. What type of humorous material does the audience expect from you? Controversial? Humor that pushes the envelope? Safe, feel-good, funny stories? Satire? Tongue-in-cheek anecdotes?

6. What image do you want your material to portray? That you are a nice human being? A sarcastic individual? A down-home Southerner? A successful business person?

7. Do you tell jokes well?

8. Does your material have to fit into a particular area, such as high tech, sports, or real estate?
9. Do you deliver longer stories better than you do one-liners?
10. Do you ad lib well? Must every story be memorized word for word?
11. Can your material revolve around you, your family, and your experiences, or do you prefer to steer away from personal references?
12. Do you feel comfortable poking fun at yourself?

I have answered these questions and know exactly the type of material I need. My goal is to collect gobs of funny, clean, nontopical stories from my everyday experiences. The *funny* part should be evident. I'm a humorist. The *clean* part should also be clear. I'm not comfortable telling even slightly risqué material and my clients don't want it. Nuff said. But why *nontopical*? There are several reasons.

Topical vs Nontopical Humor

Nontopical humor—humor that stands the test of time rather than relies on knowledge of current events—is generally less risky than topical humor. With topical material, there is a gigantic chance that some members in the audience will not know what a speaker is talking about. If they do know, they may not agree with the speaker's slant on the subject. Audience members can become offended, and once that happens, the rest of a speech may not matter. I play it safe and seek life-experience stories that all political parties, religious beliefs, geographic areas, ethnic origins, etc., will think are funny.

In addition, nontopical humor gives me the most return for my time investment. Perfected, ready-to-tell stories sometimes appear when least expected. They are nice—oh, so very nice. More often, however, it takes a long time for a piece of material to make it into speeches. This requires repeated telling and polishing to get the punch lines and timing down pat. With all that work, I want it to be in my Big Bag of speech material for years.

Most of us cannot compete with comedians who appear on our television screens nightly. They have a horde of comedy writers who specialize in topical humor. These creative geniuses come up with material so quickly, usually the day something occurred, that by the time I work up a vignette or quip on the same idea for my speech three days later, it is an old topic to my audience.

My goal is to find funny, clean, nontopical material that can be perfected, finely tuned, and used for years.

Humor hint: If you can project a story five years in the future and it's still funny, it's probably a candidate for your Big Bag. If you have to explain too much ("When this happened, the such-and-such incident had just occurred in Washington, etc."), it may be too topical.

❂ ❂ ❂

Former President George Bush was on a convention program the day before I was to speak, and I went in early in hopes of meeting him. I didn't, but I did hear his presentation.

During his remarks, he commented about his recent parachute jump and pointed out that before that event, he hadn't parachuted since September 2, 1944. The audience loved it when he poked fun at himself and added, "And I hadn't been in a free fall since the campaign of ninety-two."

Why did he parachute at age seventy-two? He declared it was a bar bet, one he had made with Clinton during the election. The loser parachuted out of a plane over Arizona. The winner jumped off of Greg Norman's porch.

A good story? It was for the time. The Canadian audience roared. My friends thought it was hilarious during a dinner party at my home the next weekend. (I told it, not George.) But this is an example of a topical piece of material. A year later my friends would have been nodding slowly until someone said, "Don't you remember? President Clinton had that hurt leg. You know, from jumping off Greg Norman's porch."

When I heard President Bush tell this piece of material, it was several months after his well-publicized parachute jump and a week after President Clinton fell off Greg Norman's porch and wound up on crutches. The parachute jump had been alluded to in the speech introduction, and the audience was seeing daily news clips of President Clinton hobbling.

The longer this book is in print, the less humorous that story will become. The facts won't be fresh. The teller will have to explain too much for the audience to get it. The explanation will take away the surprise ending.

By the way, President Bush's follow up to the story is an example of why it's good to study old joke books, although I seriously doubt if the teller in this case did the studying. He twisted an old joke (straight from dozens of old joke books) and it worked well.

He said his instructions were to jump, count to five, and pull rip cord number-one. If nothing happened, he was to pull rip cord number-two. If that one didn't work, he was to then pull rip cord number-three. If the parachute didn't open by that point, somebody should buzz Al Gore, wake him up, and alert him to get ready to go to a funeral.

Way to go George! They loved it!

Because I know exactly what type of material works for me, I can find it. You can do the same. Determine what type of material you need and stay focused. After you have that information, it's time to start using the LAWS of finding humor from your life experiences.

Chapter 5

L-LOOK AND LISTEN

My all-time favorite television show is *The Andy Griffith Show*. I'm a big fan. ("Aw, *big* ain't the word for it.") In one episode, everybody's favorite deputy Barney Fife rocks back on his heels and explains smugly to Sheriff Taylor that he's a "trained noticer." That's exactly what you become when you obey the Look and Listen law. You become a trained noticer.

From this day forth, resolve to act like a trained noticer:

- Eavesdrop when you stand in line at the grocery store.
- Search for creative headlines and true funny stories when you read newspapers.
- Make mental notes at what brought forth laughter when you eat with the gang.
- Watch people find their seats and spill their drinks and get upset when you sit in the stands before the game begins.
- Observe the other passengers when you wait to board a plane.
- Be aware if humorous conversation surfaces when you meet with a client.

The list could go on and on, but you get the idea. Become a trained noticer. Look! Listen! Notice!

When I left teaching and went into professional speaking on a full-time basis, most of my material revolved around being in pageants and being tall; funny stuff that had served me well for years. It was time to branch out. I needed a wider assortment of stories in my Big Bag, and finding them became top priority. I looked and listened for material, and I'll be dogged if it didn't pop up all around me!

A few people say that funny stuff doesn't happen around them. They contend that because I am a humorist, it only happens around me. (Now there's a scary thought.) I don't think so.

Funny speech and writing material is happening around everybody. Look and listen for it. It's everywhere. Be a trained noticer and find it.

Doin' More'n One Thang at a Time

If you're a time management, type A individual, you should be happy about now. Looking and listening do not consume any of what you consider your valuable, productive time. Not one little drop of it. Of course, I believe that any time spent gathering good speech material is valuable and productive, but I understand your reasoning. You need good stories, but finding them cannot be an all-consuming task.

The good news is that you can carry on your daily routine and still keep your eyes and ears open for humor, thus making excellent use of your time. There, don't you feel better? My seminar friends would call this multitasking. Where I live, we just call it *doin' more'n one thang at a time*.

Try these suggestions to get you in the habit of looking and listening for the funny stuff and doin' more'n one thang at a time:

- Keep a humor journal.
  The best way to develop the habit of looking and listening for humor is to keep a humor journal. Keeping a journal makes you accountable because you have to fill in spaces and answer questions. We'll discuss humor journals in the next section.
- Work with humor buddies.
  Tell the world! Or at least tell receptive friends what you're doing and ask for help. Agree that when you talk or see each other you will tell something humorous you've seen or heard. Ask your buddies to act as scouts for you, and be receptive when they bring in stories or one-liners. Ask them to check on you and to inquire how your search for humor is going. My husband and I do this routinely, and I also work with my secretary, Toni, and with several friends who are not speakers. All of our humor levels have soared to new heights.
- Put *finding humor* on your to-do list.
  Everybody keeps some sort of a to-do list. Add *find humor* to your daily list, and don't mark it off until you get results. When you have established the habit of finding one item, write *find three funny things*. A speaker once told me that it is unnecessary to write this down. Just the reminder to be on the lookout for humor was enough for him.
  Wrong!
  It is imperative to add find humor to your list so the reminder stares you in the face every time you look at the list.

Laughter from Looking and Listening

Following are several stories I gathered by keeping my eyes and ears open and doin' more'n one thang at a time.

✿ ✿ ✿

I had already boarded a flight out of Fort Lauderdale when the gate agent came aboard to talk to the man seated across the aisle from me. The agent told the passenger that upon checking his ticket they discovered his reservation was for the twenty-fifth, the next day. The man reacted instantly and slammed down the newspaper he was reading. "That secretary! Another mistake! She cannot do anything right!" His voice carried halfway through the plane. "This is the last straw!" he spat out, stuffing paper in his briefcase.

The gate agent quickly assured him there was no problem. Seats were available on this and his connecting flight, just not the seats that he thought he had been assigned. The agent gave him his new seat assignments and left.

Out of the corner of my eye, I could see this fellow just sitting there, thinking. In a few minutes, he quietly gathered his things and headed for the front of the plane. As he passed the door, a flight attendant said, "Everything's been worked out, sir. The gate agent switched your ticket to today."

Subdued, the man mumbled, "Well, actually, I've thought about it, and I'm not supposed to be going until tomorrow."

✿ ✿ ✿

On a trip into Tulsa, two flight attendants were discussing where they wanted to eat dinner that night. They had heard of a restaurant called the Cajun Wharf but didn't know where it was located. A passenger told them he had heard it was great, but he couldn't help them with directions. They asked several other people for the information to no avail.

Finally, one of the attendants clicked on the intercom and said, "Attention, ladies and gentlemen. If anyone on board knows the location of the restaurant in Tulsa named the Cajun Wharf, please raise your hand." Several hands shot up. "Thank you," she said, and proceeded up the aisle to get the information.

A very excited woman several rows in front of me touched the attendant on the arm when she passed and said, "Excuse me, Miss, but would you mind asking if anybody knows the name of a good, cheap motel?"

❂ ❂ ❂

The plane didn't have telephones, but the rude passenger across the aisle from me kept insisting to the flight attendant that he be allowed to use the special phone on board for airline personnel. He needed to make a car reservation. She told him several times there was no such telephone, but he was adamant. He was a million miler at the platinum level; he knew the plane had a secret telephone.

Finally, she gave in. "Sir, you are correct. We do have a telephone on board. It's usually just for airline personnel, but if your car reservation is that important, I'll let you use it. Which rental agency do you want to call?"

He puffed out his chest and responded, "Hertz." She left, supposedly to place the call. He gave the passengers around him a they-know-better-than-to-fool-with-me look.

Minutes later she returned and told him that she had Hertz on the line. He followed her to the front of the plane, and she handed him the intercom, which resembled a telephone receiver. Putting it to his ear, he heard a flight attendant in the back of the plane say "Hertz Rental Car." With a smug smile, he made his reservation.

Two flight attendants in the back of the plane and one at the front could barely work the remainder of the flight for laughing. I'm not so sure about the people at the Hertz counter when he landed!

Places to look and listen:

Car pools

Club meetings

Golf matches

Dinner parties

Lines (bank, post office, airport)

The local mall

The office lounge, coffee pot

Church, choir practice

Meetings

Cleaners, grocery stores, hardware stores, etc.

Sporting events

Children's activities

Social occasions

Anywhere and everywhere!

Chapter 6

Every woman who has ridden aimlessly with an obviously lost male driver has thought or said what the *A* in LAWS represents. "Why don't you just *ask?*"

People love to tell their funny stories. They just need a little prodding from an eager listener. Trained noticers prod and listen. Following are several ways to ask that worked for me.

Be Direct

Directly asking people to tell you something funny that has happened to them is a great way to find life-experience stories. To a fellow passenger, say, "Tell me something funny that's happened to you on a plane?" To a cab driver, say, "What's the funniest thing that has happened in your cab?" To a hotel clerk, say, "Tell me something humorous you've seen when people check in."

Before my friends go on vacation or to a convention, I ask them to "bring back a funny story for me." I consider it a compliment when an acquaintance tells me that something funny happened on a trip and she thought of me. Like panning for gold, I sometimes sift through a lot of weak replies, but finding a nugget is worth it.

I gathered the following stories by directly asking for humor:

❁ ❁ ❁

One flight attendant I asked to tell me something funny said she couldn't think of anything. Within minutes, however, she returned, grinning from ear to ear.

On another flight, the attendants reluctantly took turns waiting on an uppity woman who offended every person who tried to help her. Nothing suited the woman, and with each complaint, she hit her call button. Ding! There was not enough overhead space. Ding! She did not get the seat she wanted. Ding! Ding! Ding! The plane was too hot. Have the captain turn down the heat. The flight attendants were taking turns waiting on her, and the plane hadn't even left the ground.

When they were finally in the air, they served dinner, which consisted of beans, a piece of chicken, and a baked potato wrapped in aluminum foil. Within seconds, the annoying woman pushed the button yet again—Ding!—and told the flight attendant, "This is a bad potato."

The attendant picked up the potato and spanked it three times. "Bad, bad, bad potato!"

❁ ❁ ❁

I asked a taxicab driver in Spartanburg, South Carolina, what was the funniest thing that had happened in his cab. He mulled the question around in his mind a few seconds and drawled, "It coulda been that time I had that hawg as a fare?"

"A hog? Like a big pig?"

"Yeah, a hawg. *H-A-W-G*. Hawg."

He told me that a fellow wanted to get a "hawg" down to his brother in Cowpens, South Carolina, and didn't have time to take it. A cab seemed like the solution. My driver hadn't much wanted to do it, but he started thinking and decided that "a fare's a fare."

Apparently, it took the two men working together to get the huge hog into the backseat. The hog had a big snout and pointy, floppy ears—and it didn't want to ride in a cab. The animal spread its feet up against the door frame and fought them all the way. Finally, the men got the hog in the backseat, and, according to my driver, "me and hawg was off."

Once they started moving along, the hog managed to get up on the backseat and look out the side windows. People were running off the road, going into ditches. The driver pulled up at a traffic light, and a woman in the next lane rolled down her window and started pounding on her dash and pointing to get the driver's attention. "Hey! Mister! There's a hog in your backseat!"

I asked him if he would do it again, and his response was quick.

"Nope. Not again," he said, shaking his head.

I leaned forward. "It messed up your cab, didn't it?"

"Naw, that wasn't it atall," he explained. "The thing is, hawgs don't tip."

Then he caught my eye in the rearview mirror and grinned. "But ladies do."

❂ ❂ ❂

A hotel driver named Stewart met me at the New Orleans airport, and seconds after I settled into the long, black car, I asked, "How long have you been driving for the Hyatt?"

He looked out his side window as he maneuvered into traffic. Without glancing my way, he casually replied, "Oh, several years."

I waited a few seconds, then asked, "What's the funniest thing that has happened to you driving people back and forth?"

Stewart cocked his head to one side and looked at me in the rearview mirror. Studying me between glances at the road, he finally answered a block later. "The funniest thing is, that is the same question you asked me when I drove you about a year ago."

Ask Questions That Lead to Humorous Answers

If being direct takes folks off guard, word questions to get the conversation going and pull out a humorous response. Rather than "What's the funniest thing you've had happen checking people into the hotel?" say "What's the largest number of people you've caught staying in one room?"

Instead of "What changes have you seen in coaching?" try "What did you think the first time a football player came to school wearing an earring?"

In place of "Tell me something funny that's happened being a flight attendant?" try "What's the oddest thing you've seen someone try to carry on a plane?"

Think of it as making taffy. (Oh, boy. Now there's something we do often in today's world.) Word questions to get the conversation going and pull-l-l-l out the story.

Let People Tell Their Stories

In our eagerness to tell our story, we sometimes toe tap while others get through theirs. We don't key in because we're thinking of how to spring forth when it is our turn. Be receptive to hearing somebody's funny story even if you think you know where they're headed. I want to hear anybody's story, almost anytime. I hang around after every speech and let others have the floor. That's where I got the following story.

❀ ❀ ❀

After a speech for the Iowa School Boards Association, a shorter, slightly balding gentleman stepped forward and gazed up at me. Hearing me speak had brought back a memory, and he wanted to share it.

He officiated for high school girls' basketball in Iowa. At the state playoffs one year, a team had a player who was about my height, six feet two inches. In the third quarter of a close game, he called a foul on her. When he blew the whistle and signaled in her direction, the teenager spun around and glared at him. People in the stands froze. The referee sensed that she was going to do the wrong thing, but he was incorrect. She slowly smiled and said, "Okay. You got me. Good call." She handed the official the ball and, as she passed him, reached down and patted him on the top of the head. The fans roared approval. He let it go.

The game got closer in the last minutes, and at a crucial point the referee called another foul on the tall, young star. This time, however, she disagreed, and there was no hint of a smile. As a matter of fact, when she wheeled around, fire was in her eyes. For an instant, the man in charge thought she was going to blow up. But no, with an inner strength, perhaps fueled by the desire to stay in the game, the athlete mustered restraint. With the crowd watching every move, she smiled through gritted teeth and mumbled, "I do not agree, but it's your whistle." The referee moved toward the scorer's table, and seconds later the young player again played to the fans when she walked by and patted him on the head a second time. He definitely was not thrilled but, with seconds left in the competition, chose to ignore it again.

The moment the final horn sounded, the officials headed to the referees' locker room, where the man telling me the story eventually looked in the mirror. There on the top of his head were two wads of chewing gum.

Set Up Humor Hunts

After you get the hang of directly asking leading questions, you might want to graduate to more planned activities and go for bigger game. Try humor hunts. These are planned events or activities where the main purpose is to ask for stories. A secondary purpose is to have fun. Here are several ideas with proven positive results.

Solicit Stories for a Specific Purpose

When I was invited to speak at Auburn University to mark the hundred-year anniversary of women at the school, I wanted to use stories that were directly related to the Auburn experience. I had plenty of stories from when I was a student (and I was there almost a decade), but very few stories from other times.

With the help of relatives in the Auburn area, women from every era back to the twenties were invited to come together one morning and tell me funny stories from their Auburn days. Six weeks before the program, I went to Alabama for the "Humor Tea," where we laughed for hours and I got enough speech material for three programs.

On the big day, my contributors had reserved seats, and I made sure the audience knew they had supplied much of the material. From my view on stage, I could see each one of their faces as I told something that they had contributed. When the speech was completed, other women rushed forward to tell me their stories. It was a neat humor hunt that worked for that occasion and, quite honestly, added immensely to my Big Bag of stories. Following are a couple of examples that came from that hunt.

❂ ❂ ❂

Miss Katharine Cater served as Dean of Women at Auburn University for, well, it seemed like forever. Generations of Auburn women both respected this outstanding woman and, quite honestly, feared her in a nice sort of way. She practically ruled the lives of those of us who attended college when young women still checked in and out of the dorm according to certain hours. If we missed a curfew, we were restricted to our rooms. Few explanations were accepted. One can understand, therefore, how quickly the next occurrence spread around the campus.

During the sixties, the officers of the Women's Student Government Association and Dean Cater attended a meeting in Birmingham and, lo and behold, had a flat tire on the way back to Auburn. While they stood on the side of the highway trying to decide what to do, one of the students (surely a graduating senior) couldn't resist a comment. "You see, Dean Cater. You can too have a flat tire on the way back to the dorm."

❂ ❂ ❂

Caroline, a pharmacy graduate from the seventies, told about the time she and several of her friends were invited to a fraternity formal with an antebellum theme. The gowns for the affair were to be ordered by the fraternity from Bellingrath Gardens in Mobile. All the girls needed to do to obtain a correctly-sized gown was to turn in their measurements to their dates in a sealed envelope.

Turn in their measurements? Sure. The girls smelled a whole fraternity of rats. What group of college guys would resist glancing at the measurements of their dates before the information was mailed? The suspicious young women surmised that their measurements would be posted on the fraternity house bulletin board. Of course, the boys professed indignation at the mere suggestion of impropriety and assured their dates that the vital statistics would be sent straight to Mobile without the envelopes being opened. No brothers would see the numbers.

The young women turned in the information, and within twenty minutes the measurements were posted.

But Caroline and her friends had outsmarted their dates. They had been creative with their statistics. Unfortunately, this meant that when the gowns arrived, each was too big at the bust.

The report was that when they fast danced, the gowns faced forward even when the girls turned from side to side.

Have a Humor Party

The Auburn experiment worked so well, that several years later, I tried a variation of it. A friend of mind, Norma, was going to Alabama with me for a speech and we used the opportunity to set up a Storytelling Party. My Aunt Carolyn, the best storyteller in our family, handled the details and hosted the event. Her friends came and brought stories with them.

Along with the time, location, and hostess's name, the printed invitation read:

It's Story Time!!!
Bring a funny story
to share with
Jeanne Robertson
and
Norma White

They came. And they brought funny stories. For example:

Clearing her to-do list was of utmost importance for Mrs. Edwards, a friend's mother in Auburn, Alabama. The Southern lady had become very much to the point and slightly impatient in her later years. She still had to have things done correctly, but *right away.*

During Christmas her daughter Carol called to tell her there was a visitor on the way. "Mama, Jane Moore is coming out to see you and is bringing a poinsettia."

The hard-of-hearing older woman shouted into the phone, "WHO?"

"Jane Moore, Mama. She is coming to see you and bringing a poinsettia."

"BRINGING A WHAT?"

"A poinsettia."

At that, the woman slammed down the phone and left her daughter with a dial tone on the other end.

Within the hour, Jane Moore arrived and handed the elderly woman the Christmas flower. Mrs. Edwards took the poinsettia and said, "Thank you, and here!" and thrust the obligatory thank-you note back at her.

Make the Amateur Storyteller a Star

Tom Parham is a prolific storyteller, but he never gets anything down on paper. After years of pushing him to put his favorites in writing, I gave up. It wasn't going to happen. One night, with several of us in attendance who had heard the stories a number of times through the years, Tom retold every story any of us could remember. If he left out anything, we reminded him. (It's funny how listeners key in on something the first time they hear a story that the teller may later forget.)

I put all of Tom's stories in the word processor. He then could have hard copies to give to his sons, and I had stacks of new stories that Tom said I was free to use. Many of the stories weren't speech material, but a few certainly were. As with the women in Auburn, I make sure Tom gets credit.

❀ ❀ ❀

Tom had a friend, Al, whose daddy umpired high school baseball games. "He was a crook, no question about it," Tom always recalled with a shake of his head.

Al Jr. was batting in a crucial ninth-inning situation in a game where his daddy was umpiring. He had two strikes and two balls when the pitcher threw one right down the middle of the plate. Al Jr. took it standing still. He never twitched an eyelid. It was clearly the young man's third strike, but nepotism reared its head.

Al Sr. threw his hand in the air and with his best umpiring voice boomed, "BALL THREE!" Then, under his breath he added, "But if another one comes along like that, boy, you'd better take a whack at it."

❀ ❀ ❀

Tom also tells the story of Roma Boykin, a legendary pitcher from Rock Ridge, North Carolina. Roma was what was respectfully called a "big-league local." He was the top baseball dog in the county in his day, with all the perks that accompany such an unofficial title.

Word spread about him. Roma finally got his chance at the majors and went up to show off his stuff. His call came from the Philadelphia A's. That was when the legendary Connie Mack was the manager and sat in a rocking chair alongside the field and watched the goings on. Roma had no idea who he was. He had never seen a lot of old men in rocking chairs out on baseball fields, but it was the majors. What did he know?

North Carolina boy Roma was out there pitching in the third inning—his first day in the majors–and Connie Mack got up and walked out to the mound to give a little advice. When he finished, Roma spit out a wad of tobacco juice and said, "Now, old man, I do the pitching. You sit back in the chair and rock."

The next day, they sent Roma back home to Rock Ridge, North Carolina.

Make It Easy for People to Share Humor

A good friend, Liz Curtis Higgs from Louisville, Kentucky, is one of the busiest speakers and authors around. Her speaking calendar is always booked solid several years out. Her books include *Help, I'm Laughing and I Can't Get Up: Fall-Down Funny Stories to Fill Your Heart and Lift Your Spirit* and *One Size Fits All and Other Fables*.

As many speakers have, Liz found that audience members like to tell her their stories, and she sure likes listening. But she has taken her gathering to a new level of humor hunting. She puts a letter in the back of the meeting room that encourages people to send her funny stories. She forwards a little gift when they do, and if she uses a story in a publication, she sends the contributor an autographed copy of the book.

I did a similar thing in my last book, *Mayberry Humor Across the USA*. The book shows clearly that the type of humor that has made *The Andy Griffith Show* popular for so many years is still out there. To illustrate my point, I told true stories I had gathered from all over the country. In the closing section, I invited readers to share Mayberry-type stories with me and gave out my address. That was all the enticement Lamar Gilson in South Carolina needed.

❁ ❁ ❁

Lamar wrote to tell me of the time her husband Mark, a retired physician, worked with the Lions Club Sight Van, going around to different locations. Mark worked the tonometer, an instrument used for testing glaucoma by measuring the pressure. He was training another member named Pete to use the tonometer, and Pete was having a really difficult time getting a reading on one old-timer.

The elderly man had been instructed to keep very still and quiet and was following instructions to the letter, sitting there absolutely immobile. Finally, the trainee said, "Doc, I can't get anything here." Mark went over and tried, with no success. The patient remained calm and continued to do as he had been told, sitting there like a piece of stone, not moving a muscle while the two men fiddled with the machine for several minutes.

Finally, the doctor decided that maybe the machine needed adjustment. He and Pete were still tinkering with the piece of equipment and debating what to do when the old man, by then resembling a statue, murmured, "It's glass."

Minutes later the man stood to leave, completely oblivious to the confusion he had caused, and said, "You boys ever want to hunt deer come on up to my place. We got plenty of 'em." And he left.

Wear a Button

When fellow NSA member Rebecca Morgan in San Jose, California, was writing a book on customer service, she told me she wore a button with the words ASK ME ABOUT CUSTOMERS

FROM HELL. Well, that gave me an idea, and I had a button made with TELL ME A FUNNY STORY.

❂ ❂ ❂

The first two times the waitress approached my table, she didn't see my TELL ME A FUNNY STORY button. On her third stop, I turned around in my chair so she couldn't miss it. "Tell you a funny story?" she read slowly. Her look alone could have stopped a stampeding herd. Then she spoke. "So, what do I have to do now? Entertain *and* serve?"

Interview People

Everybody knows some characters. Spend time with them. In most cases they are thrilled someone will listen and laugh with them. Even if you don't get a great story, you'll have a delightful afternoon.

Around the time of the sixtieth anniversary of the Miss North Carolina Pageant, I went to Greensboro to spend the greater portion of a day with Ruth Covington Thomas, the first Miss North Carolina.

Ruth won the title of Miss North Carolina in 1937 when she was fifteen years old, even though the rules were definite that the contestants had to be seventeen. "Oh, so you lied?" I inquired. She grinned and said, "Absolutely not. I just signed my name." At the Miss America Pageant, she went on to explain, the pageant officials sent Miss South Carolina home because she was too young. Ruth said, "Again, I just kept my mouth shut."

When Ruth returned to North Carolina, having come in third to Miss America, someone found out she was underage, and pageant officials wrote that they were coming to get her trophy. Ruth didn't keep her mouth shut then. She told them, "You just try."

There was another surprise for Ruth in Atlantic City. All she had to do to win in Charlotte was parade around in a swimsuit, but in the national competition, she was informed that she needed to have talent. Recalling it sixty years later, the singer and dancer shimmied her shoulders and said, "I told them, 'You're in luck. I've got talent!'"

Right before I left, I told her I hoped a Miss North Carolina would reminisce with me when it had been sixty years since I won the crown. She looked up from her wheelchair, gave a beauty-pageant smile, and said, "I will."

The most memorable line of the day, however, came when I asked Ruth what she did when she didn't win the title of Miss America. She flashed that smile again and said, "I entered the ninth grade."

Hunting Rules:

- Be up front about what you're doing.
- Double check later for permission to tell.
- When putting someone's story in writing, let the person approve the copy.
- Always give credit when it's due.
- Never pretend someone else's story happened to you.

Warning! Asker Beware! Danger!

"I swear. It happened. I saw it with my own eyes!"

"Well, I didn't actually see it, but..."

When you ask for humor, there is always the risk that what people tell you happened to them or Aunt Bertha on her Las Vegas trip in reality didn't happen to either one of them. I now have a story about the number of people who have sworn to me they know the woman from the small town who was in a big city hotel and dropped to the elevator floor when the large man with a dog got on and said, "Hit four." Apparently, this little old lady moves around a lot and lives in thousands of small towns.

The truth is that when it comes to telling stories, good-hearted, honest people will lie. Actually, the word *lie* is a little strong. Perhaps *stretch, exaggerate,* or *embellish* is more accurate. You ask for a story and they want to make you happy, so they tell you something and say it happened to them or their cousin. If pinned down, yes, they eventually say, maybe they heard it at a speech or on TV. They may be totally unaware they're not telling the truth. After all, they got the story from a sales associate who heard it from the cousin of an ex-husband. Firsthand, by golly!

Askers beware! Especially aspiring speakers. It is not a problem when someone incorrectly claims that a story happened to them or to so-and-so. Nosiree, bob, that is not a problem. The danger develops when you as a speaker or writer take the story and then say that it happened to you. That's where you wind up with egg on your face. The following personal experience provides a perfect illustration.

After my speech to a school system in Florida, an administrator told me a funny story that happened in her classroom when she taught the first grade. I knew it would be perfect to tell in several situations, and so I asked if it had really happened in her class. Yes. Would she mind if I told it? No. What was her name so I could give her credit if I used it? She told me she didn't want credit. If I could use it, I could have it. Most people sincerely mean that, but once in a while, this is a clue.

Back home, I told the story to my husband, a former elementary principal. We both thought it would be perfect to tell the next week when I spoke to the Michigan Elementary and Middle School Principals Association. One of my points was to look for the true humor happening around them every day.

I am a physical education major who practice-taught on the elementary level. It would have been easy to say the story happened in my class during that time. It would also have been easy to say the story happened in my husband's school when he was a principal. Both were tempting. But why? The truth was that it didn't happen to us.

The next week when I was making the point that humor happens around us every day, I began the story with "I was in Florida last week, and a former elementary teacher told me about a little boy in her class who didn't know how to tell time." The audience reacted instantly. People cut their eyes at one another. Had they heard the story? I stopped and said to a women seated at the front, "Y'all have heard this." She grinned and replied, "Yesterday. The president of our national association told it in her speech."

My reaction? I quickly said, "The woman in Florida lied! She lied! She said it happened to her. No wonder she wouldn't give me her name!" It was hilarious. I went on to say that if any of them wanted to tell me a story after the speech, they had to take a lie detector test.

With the national president speaking at all the state conventions, this story was flying through elementary school circles. What if I had opened the story by saying it had happened in my classroom or my husband's school? I would have lost credibility. My stomach tightens to think about it. They would have still enjoyed me, but they would have looked at me from a different perspective and been suspicious of the rest of my stories when I said they happened to me.

This all leads to an important question. When someone tells you a story and swears it really happened to them, how do you know if it did or didn't?

The answer is simple. You never know if it really happened to them, but you always know if it happened to you.

So beware of hearing a funny story and saying that it happened to you.

Humor hint: Refrain from saying statements like "Now this story is true" or "This story really happened." Comments like these say to the audience that the rest of your stories are fabricated.

Chapter 7

W−WRITE UP

We are halfway through the LAWS of gathering humorous stories from your life experiences. By now you know it's important to become a trained noticer who diligently *looks, listens,* and *asks* for material in everyday experiences.

But what do you do when you see, hear, or receive a story or an idea? You observe the *W* in LAWS. As quickly as possible, *write up*! If you don't, you will find yourself doing what I did. Wondering about the Boston Celtics.

The Boston Celtics...

You are probably reading this because you have a need for funny illustrations. And, like me, you have a system for collecting ideas. Maybe you've been tossing articles into files for years or listing ideas on the nearest wad of paper.

I have tablets of ideas—long lists of words to remind me of funny stories or ideas. As a matter of fact, I have collected some of the best story ideas a speaker could ever hope for.

Gotta be award-winning stuff. If only I knew what they were. That leads me back to the Boston Celtics.

In big letters on one of my lists are the words *Boston Celtics*. The words are surrounded by stars, which I typically use to indicate a really hot idea. My handwriting. My stars. My great idea. But looking at them from a much later date, the words are cold from setting so long on the tablet, and they mean nothing to me. I have absolutely no idea what the funny story was. I've racked my brain, and the Celtics aren't in there. I should have *written up*.

The Difference Between Writing Up and Jotting Down

There is a big difference between writing *up* and jotting *down*, and you will do both extensively when gathering life-experience material.

Jotting down means putting a few words on paper to remind us of something later. Sometimes we jot down on tablets, sometimes in our computers, but more often we jot down on scraps of paper or margins of whatever is handy.

Writing up means putting down more than a couple of words to remind us of what occurred. It means taking the time to write up a more detailed account of the story. Writing up involves sentences. It involves paragraphs. It involves vignettes like the short anecdotes in *Readers Digest* that we often read first. Fortunately, writing up does *not* require instant, correct punctuation. Hallelujah!

The Importance of Writing Up

The goal is to collect a large supply of stories, not long lists of possibilities that we try to finalize at a later date. It's darned difficult to get back at that later date and carry long lists of ideas to fruition. If we can't find time when a story happens, it's highly unlikely we'll find time months later. The task would be monumental. We may bring several ideas to story form, but a lot of funny stuff will get away.

A few words on a list get cold. If we are able to recall what those few words meant months later, the spontaneity of what happened is gone. The exact wording that made it funny is lost in the dustbin of history. Oh, heck, you'll probably wad up the piece of paper and throw it in the trash can. Writing up as soon as possible captures the magic.

You may be thinking, "Oh no! I'm in trouble. I am not a writer." Come on now. You're after the humorous story, not the Pulitzer. Just say to yourself what occurred as though you were telling it to a friend. Think who, where, when, and what happened, and start writing. Sure, you'll perfect it later, but first get it in written up form.

To ease apprehension, remember that when writing up:

- Nothing is carved in stone.
- You can always change what you write.
- There are no grades on punctuation.
- Practice makes it faster and easier.
- Nobody ever has to see it. (Hip hip hooray!)

The Necessity of Jotting Down

If you are thinking that you won't jot down anymore, read on. You jot down. You jot and jot and jot down. You need to scatter pencils and jotting-down tablets throughout your home and office. You need to locate them near every telephone. You need to put them in your car so that you can jot down before getting out or revving up the engine to leave.

Lest you forget, however, you jot down only to remember something until you get to the journal to write up. (Isn't this fun?) Meetings, telephone conversations, the grocery store, standing in line anywhere. When something happens, jot it down, but then write it up as soon as possible.

If you don't jot things down when they happen, a lot of good ideas get away. If you don't write up your stories soon after, a lot of good stories never materialize.

Chapter 8

S—STRETCH IT

For the *S* in LAWS, let's go back to Mayberry for a minute. In one of the episodes, Sheriff Andy Taylor attempts to downplay to Miss Crump what he did to get Opie and his friends to study history. He says, "I just, uh, kinda told 'em a little tale...well, you know, put a little extra jam on the bread."

Sheriff Taylor would make an excellent speaker or writer. A lot of good, true stories just need a little extra jam spread on them. Our audiences deserve it.

Putting a Little Extra Jam on the Bread

Thankfully, plenty of stories will fall into your lap in mint condition. Andy Taylor and a truckload of jam couldn't make them any better. But some of life's humorous experiences need a slight tweak. A small amount of embellishing. A dab of jam. Officially, this is called *creative license* and should not be confused with out-and-out lying.

Stretching, taking creative license, embellishing, and downright fibbing all get a little ticklish when we're talking about life-experience humor. Basically, we're telling the audience that something happened. And, of course, sometimes it didn't happen exactly in the way we say it did.

It's easy when we use jokes. The die is cast when a story starts with "A man had this talking dog..." The teller can take that story anywhere and the audience will, in most cases, go along. But when the story starts with "I was in Philadelphia over the Fourth of July, and...," a different stage is set.

I certainly won't decree what's right and wrong in this area. In the end, every speaker has to decide what works. Each of us knows our own style of speaking and what our audiences expect. But here is my take on the subject.

In the stretching room—your mind—you might have to twist something a woman on the plane said to make it a little funnier. Help her out a little. Put her punch line at the end of her sentence. But be careful what you add. What if you say a woman was choking to death on the plane and you got up and saved her life and, aw-shucks, it was what anyone would have done? If what actually happened was that a woman was choking on the plane and another person saved her, then you would be lying rather than embellishing the story. This is a no-no.

Or what if you told a story based on the results of a survey you did and you never did that survey? Whoa.

Or what if you are detailing a heartrending story about somebody who did certain things to keep from dying, and what if the truth is that the fellow's deader than a doornail and six feet under and none of that stuff he tried worked? Uh-oh.

Audiences don't mind a little stretch. They don't even want to know when that stretch tilts more toward the fiction side. But they do mind, for example, if you say a story happened when you were a CEO somewhere and you never were. They don't mind if you make the dog that sat on your shoes a little bigger, but they'll be bothered if you say you have a Ph.D.

and you don't. (Well, you sort of have a Ph.D. You bought it through a mail order school.) And they will be bothered if you tell stories about your little girl and you don't have a little girl. What in the world?

When I tell stories about my son, I usually begin with, "My son's name is...Beaver." If I pause right there and wait on them, the audience will laugh. Several years ago, during that laugh, I added as an aside, "We have a little girl named Muskrat." That got a really big laugh. There was only one problem. At the end of the speech, person after person would ask about Muskrat. "How old is little Muskrat?" they would ask. Or, "Is Muskrat going to be tall?" Of course, then I would have to say, "Oh, I don't have a little girl. I just made that up."

I found out that when they learned there wasn't a Muskrat, they no longer believed there was a Beaver. But the line about Muskrat was such a good laugh that I didn't want to ditch it. Finally, after seeing more faces fall when I said there was no Muskrat, I switched the line to, "If we had had a little girl, we were going to name her Muskrat." It got the same amount of laughter.

You can usually detect when audiences believe you've gone too far. I have a story about a contestant in a beauty pageant who had a major problem with a baton. I saw it happen. I embellished it, and it has become a trademark story for me. Audiences and meeting planners request that I tell it. But the reason the baton story goes over so well is that it's believable. Embellished? Yes. But still believable.

I also have a story about a contestant in a beauty pageant who was playing the piano when it started rolling. This also actually happened, but when I embellished it, I had the piano rolling all the way off the stage. People didn't buy it. It's still a great story, but when that piano rolls out of view behind the curtain, I've crossed into the impossible. And when I say, "The last time we saw the piano, it was on the road to Montgomery," it's absurd. Audiences still laugh, but not the way they do with the more believable stretch on the baton story.

We're supposed to have common sense on this sort of thing. Not everybody does, of course, but I'm assuming you do. If not, announce at the beginning of your speech that everything is fiction and let her rip!

Stretching Exercises

With that little sermonette out of the way, let me share a few simple idea-stretching exercises to turn potentially funny, everyday occurrences into stories that are really funny. When I work on a story that needs a little help, I consider the situation, think one of the following, and let my mind wander:

- Wouldn't it be funny if…
- What I thought was going to happen was…
- I thought she was going to…
- What I thought he was going to say was…
- What she should have done/said was…
- I would have loved it if…

Our friends do this to us don't they? They let us finish a story and then say, "What I thought you were going to say was…" Then they say something funnier than what we said. I'm just suggesting that we do to ourselves as our friends do unto us. Ask the stretching questions above and let your creative side take over. Also try out your story in conversation and let your friends unknowingly add to it.

❂ ❂ ❂

I arrived in Winston-Salem to speak at a convention of the Southeastern Association of Area Agencies on Aging. (Saying the title is enough to age most of us.) I parked my car in the multilevel lot and then got turned around trying to find the crosswalk to the hotel.

A couple, walking hurriedly through the cars as if they knew where they were going, came into view. "Excuse me," I said, "are you going to the conference on aging?"

The woman didn't miss a step. She broke into a big smile and quipped, "Not me. I'm just taking him. He's an exhibit."

Now the truth. Everything happened exactly as I related up until the time the woman spoke. When I asked them if they were going to the conference on aging, the woman actually said, "No, but before long, I'm sure we'll be there."

When I returned to my office, I tried out the true version on my secretary, Toni. At the end, Toni said, "I thought you were going to say she was taking him to be an exhibit."

And so it grows....

Working Backward

This exercise gets close to creating from scratch, but it starts with a line from your everyday experiences.

Any funny line is a potential story. Grab it. Jot it down. Don't let it get away. Then, during creative time, put together a little story based on your life experiences that includes or leads up to that line.

One morning as I headed to check out of the Arizona Biltmore, I passed three men who were chatting in the lobby. During the quick instant that I was within earshot, I heard one of them say, "She said if I wanted a hot breakfast, I could throw a match in my cereal." I never broke stride, but knew I had a good line. I didn't know who the "she" was or whether she made up the line or got it from a book or television. I just knew it was a good line, and I saved it.

Several years later I had the opportunity to do twenty-five speeches in twenty-five cities for one company. I traveled with a group of seven men from place to place, and this meant eating breakfast with them every morning. I was having a ball, and it took only a few days to develop a routine about the amount these guys ate every day. It contained stuff like the waitress seeing us seated and quipping, "So, what do we have here? Snow White and the Seven Dwarfs?" And the first sentence the men asked after breakfast every day? "Where are we going to eat lunch?"

The end of my routine went something like: "It's not my habit to eat biscuits and gravy and pancakes and omelettes and sausage every morning. I agree with the philosophy that if you want a hot breakfast, throw a match in your cereal."

Collect the funny line. Later, work backward to build a story around it.

Working Forward

I call this exercise the *Is-that-it? Syndrome.* Sometimes a funny story coasts along and comes to a screeching halt because there is no punch line. Don't let it get away. If the premise, the idea, the concept is funny, write it up. Later, during creative time, work on the perfect ending.

I've held stories for years trying to get the right punch.

The story as I tell it: I was emceeing a pageant in Enterprise, Alabama, and an ugly stray dog walked in the back door of the auditorium, proceeded down the aisle, up the glee-club steps to the stage, and sat down next to the lectern. Why someone didn't stop him as he meandered forth will forever remain a mystery. They just didn't, and eventually there the dog was, sitting on stage.

The show stopped. People were howling, and when they quieted a little, I said to the animal, "Do you have any talent?" More laughter, which didn't stir the dog one little bit. He just moved his head from side to side to survey the audience. I couldn't resist that and said, "I agree with you. It's a pretty mangy-looking crowd." When the audience quieted down from that line, I walked, microphone in hand, toward the dog and said, "You have made the top five. Please answer this question to the best of your ability."

At that precise moment, I'll be darned if the dog didn't yawn. Yawn!

A man in the front row quipped, "And now we know what he thinks of the emcee's jokes."

The story as it happened: The dog came in, ambled down the aisle, came up on stage and sat down beside the lectern where I was speaking. People were howling. I believe I said something like, "Do you have any talent?" I had on a full-length evening gown but proceeded to pull him by the collar until I got him off stage behind the curtain. It was hilarious.

At the reception after the pageant, one person commented, "We certainly had a mangy-looking crowd." Someone else said that the bad part was that the dog looked bored. Another person said, "I think he was yawning at some of your stories."

It gets too complicated to tell what happened and then try to work in the comments I heard at the reception. I prefer to do as Sheriff Andy Taylor did and spread a little jam on the bread. That means taking the funny comments from the reception and working them into what happened on stage.

I may be alibiing, but I think audiences find this an acceptable stretch. After all, I didn't say the dog was an award-winning animal that had been lost in a storm and made his way to Alabama and found his owner in the auditorium.

Creating Characters

In my years of telling life-experience humor, I've noticed that the person telling the story can't always be the one with the clever punch line. It gets old fast to hear too many lines like "so I quipped…," "and then I told him…," or "so I chimed in and said…."

Even if you are the person who quipped the funny line that threw the luncheon crowd into hysterical laughter, it might be better to let somebody else have that line when you retell it. Many times it is more effective to make up a character and let that mythical person have the funny line.

When people sitting next to me on planes say something funny, I jot down what they say and write it up immediately. But plenty of other times I say the funny line. In those cases, when I write up I am likely to say, "A passenger across the aisle said…." It's only a little stretch, and the stratagem makes for a better speech.

Stretch with Humor Buddies

One of the most productive things I do is to spend the day with another speaker who is also working on humor. The other person is usually Linda Pulliam, a professional speaker who lives nearby. We get together with our lists of stories that need a little help and take turns tossing out ideas and stretching them.

This exercise worked so well for me that I enticed fellow humorists Robert Henry and Al Walker to join me on a humor retreat. We holed up with our spouses at the beach in the dead of winter. For three days we took turns presenting ideas in need of group embellishing. All of the group's energy went into whatever story we were working on at the time, and no matter who came up with an idea, it belonged to the person being helped at that moment. This was wonderful!

To illustrate the idea of stretching material, I'll first share a story that I am currently using. Then I'll show the story as it initially appeared on my journal sheet. You'll see how it grew.

✪ ✪ ✪

I was eating in a restaurant by myself when a teenage waitress, with pencil and tablet in hand, came sauntering up to the table and said, "Whut you want?" Those were her only words. Good customer service. Whut you want?

I said, "I'll have a Caesar salad, and I look forward to watching you prepare it at my table as the menu indicates."

She shifted her weight and looked up from her tablet as she slung a hip to one side. "Well, we don't do that anymore. We fix it in the kitchen now."

I'm looking for humor, right? I was not going to let that pass. I said, "Why?"

She shifted her weight again, "Well, they told me that if we're fixing it at the table and we get to mixin' everything around in that big bowl, and some of the lettuce falls on the floor and the customer sees it, there's nothing we can do with it then but throw it away."

The original journal entry:

Dining. I ordered a Caesar's salad in the hotel restaurant. The menu indicated that it would be prepared at the table, but the waitress said they no longer did that because lettuce kept falling on the floor and "people see it." I guess if people see it fall, the lettuce has to be thrown away.

Here is another journal entry that preceded the story's use in my book *Mayberry Humor Across the USA*.

From Jeanne's Journal, 1986 (remember, punctuation and correct grammar don't count on the journal—it's presented here as I wrote it up):

> The association executive lined the head table people up with a bullhorn before a big banquet. "So-and-so behind so-and-so!' he blared, and slowly went through his list. "Jeanne Robertson behind so-and-so!" When he got us all lined up he went to the front of the line with his bullhorn and blared back at us, "Follow me!" We did, through a maze of rooms, into the ballroom, up the steps to the head table on the dais, where we discovered our places were in totally different order. It was like fruit basket turnover. As we bumped into each other, the man was continuously shouting directions at us through that bullhorn.

Here is the story as it appeared in *Mayberry Humor Across the USA* in a comparison to Deputy Barney Fife:

> It gave new meaning to the term "bullheadedness." The quiet, private reception for the head table dignitaries was abruptly interrupted when someone on "the committee" clicked on a bullhorn. That is right. Dressed in his best suit at a very nice reception during a state convention, the man whipped out an emergency department bullhorn, flipped the button and jolted years off our lives. "May I have your attention,

please!" he suddenly boomed. He got it. People jumped.

"Attention! Attention! It is time to proceed to the ballroom. First, we will line up in the order in which we will be seated. So-and-so behind so-and-so! Then so-and-so followed by so-and-so," he blared, methodically going down his clipboard. People did as instructed, and after a while, "Next is the speaker, Jeanne Robertson. Jeanne Robertson!" I quickly stepped into position. Everyone was happy, so throughout the room they stifled laughter, fell into place, and paid the bullhorn respect.

When we were lined up and scared to speak for fear of being reprimanded, our drill sergeant moved to the front to double-check everything. When he turned toward us again, people flinched backwards in anticipation. "Follow me!" he bellowed, the megaphone amplifying his words in our direction. I was reminded of a certain deputy shouting directions through his bullhorn in "Barney and the Cave Rescue." "Approach the cave entrance slowly. Slowly! Do not panic. Do not panic!"

Resembling a caterpillar inching along, the people assigned to the head table wound our way through the hotel corridors until we arrived at the ballroom entrance. The drill instructor with the bullhorn stopped at the door and let us pass as he watched over us every minute and continued to repeat last minute instructions. "Approach the room slowly. Slowly! Stay in line. Just follow the one in front of you. Stay in line! Keep going until the one in front of you stops! You will be at your assigned seat at the table. Stay in line!!"

(The man clearly needed to be nipped in the bud.) Someone mumbled, "For Pete's sake, you are gonna burst my ear drum with that thing." Respect for the bullhorn was dwindling.

The thousand people attending the convention stood as we entered the large hall, and they watched in polite silence as we moved up the steps of the stage to the long head table. Seconds later, they burst out laughing when we discovered we were lined up exactly backwards from our place cards.

The first person walked to the end of the table, saw it was not his seat, and turned back to look for his card. He bumped into the woman behind him, and it was like a pileup on a California freeway. People bounced off one another like beach balls as they tried to sort out the whole mess and find their assigned seats. "You are over here." "You are at the other end." "Does anyone see my name?" After a minute of sustained chaos, someone mumbled, "We are playing Fruit Basket Turnover. Sit down anywhere. We will just swap place cards." The audience roared.

Someone joked under his breath, "What we need is a good bullhorn." No sooner were the words out of his mouth when, "Just take a seat! Take any seat!" Water shook in glasses. Waiters ran out of the kitchen. The drill instructor had joined us on stage and was standing in front of the head table with that horn. pointed in our direction again.

"Just take…"

Suddenly, one of the men reached across the table, jerked the bullhorn out of the drill instructor's hand, and turned it back toward him, and thus the audience.

"Stop shouting at us through this blasted horn!"
So much for respect…and hooray for bud nipping!

Stories grow when you tell them. A twist of a word here. A funny phrase there. A humorous description inserted at the right time. It all adds to the product. Sometimes I tell a story that I think I have been telling in the same way for years. But listening to a tape of myself telling the original version of a story years ago makes me realize that's not so. Somehow during the repeated telling, it took on its current form. I told the story so often that it grew!

There is no correlation between how much time I spend on a story and how funny it becomes.

Below are three short journal entries that occurred during a six month time span. They are followed by a longer story that evolved by combining all three entries and stretching over time.

Jeanne's Journal entry: November 25, 1996. Most Memorable Thing. A woman from the Haw River Historical Museum (didn't know they had one) came up after my speech. She had a photo of me when I was Miss NC. Wanted to know if I knew if the gown in the photo was made of corduroy. If so, did I know if it was Cone corduroy which meant it was probably made in Haw River. They want to hang the picture in the museum. Boy did I surprise her. I told her it was corduroy, made in Haw River, and that she could have the dress if she wanted it. And the shoes.

In-town Journal entry, March 19, 1997. Phone. Gail Knauff with the Haw River Historical Society called about the corduroy gown they want to put in the museum. She said they had found half a mannequin and were working on getting the other half before my speech down there in April.

Jeanne's Journal entry: April 22, 1997. Well, I went down to Haw River tonight to officially donate the corduroy gown and shoes. They had found a whole mannequin but she had little feet and was a long way from being six-foot-two. The mayor of Haw River got on the floor to try and steer the tiny feet into my size eleven shoes and said he need a lot of stuffing to fill up the space.

This is the story that grew out of the three journal entries.

Vindicated!

I save stuff. Not valuable stuff in the financial sense of the word. Just things that bring back happy memories. I throw nothing away. My pack-rat habits have brought on much ribbing through the years, mainly from my husband. But his objections have never fazed me. I've continued to stash as though on a mission, and the day of the mission finally arrived.

Voilà! Exonerated! It feels good. Real good.

After speaking to the Graham, North Carolina, Historical Society, a woman named Gail Knauff showed me an eight-by-ten framed photograph from my Miss North Carolina days. She and her husband had recently written the history of Haw River. Now the

Knauffs and others in the community were actively involved in putting together the Haw River Historical Museum.

She had run across this photo and thought the gown I had on was made of corduroy. If I remembered the dress and it was indeed made of corduroy, did I happen to know if it was Cone Mills corduroy? That would mean it had been made at the Cone Mills plant in Haw River and that they wanted to hang the picture in the new museum. Could I help her?

Oh boy, could I help her. It was the day I had been waiting for. Yes, I told her. The dress was made of corduroy. Yes, the material had been made at the Haw River Cone Mills plant. Yes, put the photo in the museum, and—ta-da!—did she want the gown? How about the matching shoes?

Around 2:00 a.m., I located the thirty-four-year-old gown piled in with some psychedelic-looking bell-bottoms. Forty-five minutes later, the matching shoes fell out of my college physical education uniform.

Of course, things don't ever run as smoothly as they sound. In preparation for the big donation, Gail discovered that the Haw River Historical Society's mannequin had only half a body. If she had the bottom half of the thing, the bosom and shoulders of the gown would fall over to one side. If she had the top half, the skirt would bunch up around the waist. Either way, the mannequin would be shorter than six-foot-two.

By the time the donating night rolled around, however, Gail had obtained a whole body from a dress shop in Burlington.

To be accurate, and I certainly strive to be, I must report that the mannequin's feet were a little smaller than mine. When we eased her down into my shoes, ever careful not to knock off her curly blond wig, the mayor of Haw River got on the floor to steer the feet into place. Seconds later he looked up and said, "Bring me a bunch of rags. There's a whole lot of space to fill in these big shoes."

You'd think my husband would have been excited about my donation, but no. Jerry said he'd get excited when somebody took my high school clothes.

(If you're traveling through North Carolina, please do drop by the museum in Haw River. If the mannequin looks tipsy, stuff some papers in the shoes. The Historical Society would be thrilled if you used dollar bills.)

After three short journal entries that led to an extremely long story, let me point out that making a story work doesn't depend on how much time you spend developing it. The Haw River Museum story wound up being a great piece of material when I returned a year later to help them raise funds. This next story fell into place the minute it happened and required no additional time. I started using it immediately as an illustration of life-experience humor:

❂ ❂ ❂

I stopped in a convenience store on the loop around Paris, Texas, and asked one of two women behind the counter if the Paris Inn was much farther away. She said she had never heard of the Paris Inn. "We've got a

Comfort Inn and a Victoria Inn and a Holiday Inn, but, honey, we hadn't got a Paris Inn."

The woman standing beside her punched her on the arm and said, "Yes, we do. The Holiday Inn is now the Paris Inn. For Pete's sake, they've had a big sheet over the sign for two months. You oughta had known that."

The first woman wheeled around and retorted, "*I* don't do any business in hotels, so I don't have to keep up with the names."

Part III

JEANNE'S JOURNAL SYSTEM

Chapter 9

WHETTING YOUR APPETITE

Picture this:

It's the winter holiday season and you're home. It's been a great year, but you're tired and hope that as January approaches you'll have time to rejuvenate.

Your enthusiasm is desperate for a jump start. Your speeches need fresh material. You are in the planning stages for a new program because repeat engagements are on the books for the coming year. You've agreed to do an article for a magazine and want to use personal illustrations, but you are tired of the same ol', same ol' that you've used a long time.

This is a familiar scenario, but if you've been keeping your humor journal for the past year, it could continue in the following manner.

Say to your secretary, "Bring me the journal stories for the year." The computer whirls. Papers stack up in the tray and spill out onto the floor. Your secretary laughs out loud and shouts, "Some of these are pretty good." Within an hour, hundreds of humorous vignettes from your experiences over the previous twelve months are stacked on your desk. You've got your jump start.

Life is wonderful!

This scene takes place in my office every year. Perhaps it will pique your interest in my system.

What Is Jeanne's Journal System?

In a nutshell, Jeanne's Journal System is an organized way to use limited time to gather a large reserve of humorous stories from your life experiences.

This is how it works.

You have a personal journal page, handwritten or typed, that is arranged according to your daily humor-gathering opportunities. Think of the journal as a person tagging along and asking if you just saw or heard anything that could become a humorous piece of material for a speech or piece of writing.

The journal page serves as a memory jogger. But more important, you are accountable to the journal. Like a child pulling at your sleeve, your journal page asks, "Did sumphin funny just happen? Huh? Huh? Come on, Mom, tell me. Why are you laughing?" You have to answer, and your answers build your supply of humorous stories.

When you find a funny idea or story by looking, listening, or asking, jot down enough words to remember what happened until you can get to your journal page to write up the story in vignette form. The story can be stretched if necessary, either immediately or at any time.

Once you write up a story, you can stop trying to remember it. It's yours. Like coins dropped in a piggy bank, the humorous stories add up in your Big Bag and are there when you need them.

One more thing. For this to work, it may be necessary to change the way you think about gathering material.

Uh-oh. Did you say *change*?

A Major Mind Shift

It's time to think in another direction. Normally we look for humorous material to fit a specific purpose or to illustrate certain points. With the Jeanne's Journal System, this becomes secondary. Your primary objective is simply to collect a large supply of great stories.

You can do two things to shift into this mode of thinking:

1. Put *purpose* on the back burner. You no longer need to focus on what a story illustrates, when you can use it, or how you will use it. Focus instead on getting the good stories. Later you can figure out the how, the when, and the where.
2. Focus on your humor ops. (Rhymes with tops.) Politicians have photo ops. We have humor ops. Think about where and when you have opportunities to find funny material every day. These are the ways you approach your search for humor. Make these daily humor-gathering opportunities the main categories on your journal sheet.

Why Do It This Way?

The reason you gather funny stories first and decide later how to use them is that *you can't go back.*

With all humor sources other than life experiences—books, cassettes, cyberspace, newsletters, magazines, joke services—if you read or hear something funny, you can find it again later. It's always there, in print or on cassette, waiting for us to need it.

Humor from life experiences doesn't wait. It passes by and puts the burden on us to reach out, grab it, and figure out how to keep it from getting away. If we do not record the humor in some manner when it flies by, it's probably gone. This book teaches you how to grab it when it passes.

How Jeanne's Journal System Came About

Although I preferred life-experience humor from almost the beginning of my professional speaking career, I didn't develop my journal system for the first twenty years. Prior to developing my system, my habit was to find one funny story, line, or idea per day from what was happening around me. That seemed like an easy goal. I remember thinking when I set it, "Just one funny nugget every twenty-four hours? That can't be tough." My intention was to gather so much funny material that I wouldn't know what to do with it all.

Accountability appeals to me. I loved little gold stars in elementary school. So to encourage myself to meet my goal, I challenged my husband to ask every day what humorous tidbit I had found. It became a game, and Jerry was a reliable teammate. (One night when we left a dinner party he said, "Did you get anything?" People within earshot may have thought I had stuffed something in my purse.)

I felt that I was doing well in my gathering, accumulating, and showing off to Jerry. I was proud of myself. But there was a problem. Funny ideas were piling up, but new, completed stories weren't showing up in my speeches. As a matter of fact, some of them never surfaced again after the day I found them.

For years I jotted down these daily discoveries on long, yellow tablets and in big, spiral notebooks and eventually transferred them to index cards by categories. I kept spare copies and backup copies of everything. When time permitted, I pored over the papers and decided what to try in presentations. It was an extensive, complex system. The government would have loved it.

Creative time was spent hunting, reorganizing, and spinning my wheels. Beach vacations were spent wading through waves of papers. My scribbled words often made little sense. If my notes were legible and I managed to remember what happened, I couldn't recapture the comedic timing. I frantically searched through mounds of paper for a story I knew was there—somewhere. My creativity was a revolving mess.

I thought that technology would be the answer to my organizational problems, so I got my first computer in the early eighties. I learned a quick lesson: What I put in the computer is what I get out. I was putting my long, handwritten lists of ideas into the word processor and getting the same lists back out, neatly typed.

Then, in 1983, Jerry accompanied me on a speech, but stayed in the hotel room to watch Duke basketball. The game was over when I returned, and he directed his attention toward me. Had the speech gone well? Had the audience been responsive? Had I found my one funny idea for the day?

Yes, yes, and yes, the latter a one-liner made by a waiter. I had jotted it down on a paper napkin. I had met my goal.

Jerry's attention was diverted to the score, but after a while he nonchalantly asked whom I had sat beside. His question jiggled my memory, and I told him about something a hilarious woman had said. Minutes later, Jerry asked another simple question. This one led to the development of Jeanne's Journal System: "Did you jot that down too?"

Well, obviously, I had not. Unbelievably, I heard myself say, "I already had my funny idea for the day."

I hate it when someone just stares at me, especially my husband. I didn't like his next comment either. He mumbled, "You let a lot of funny stuff get away."

The nerve!

Jerry, a man who couldn't even miss a Duke ballgame to go to a banquet where his wife was speaking, was beginning to irritate me. I did what most people would do in that situation. I decided to redirect the wrongdoing.

"I realize a lot of funny stuff gets away, Jerry, but it's your fault. If you would travel with me all the time, ask me specific questions about what was funny, and encourage me to write up the answers, I'd have more funny stuff than I could ever use." (Had I gone nuts?)

"You...you want me to travel to all your speeches?"

"Yes." (Why God didn't strike me down right then for lying, I'll never know.) "I need you along to say things like `Did the cab driver say anything funny?' and `What were you and the waitress laughing about?' and `Ask the flight attendant what is so hilarious.' Then I'd have gobs of funny stuff."

The mere thought of traveling together all the time made us burst out laughing. Hotel rooms can get very small, even for people who love each other. A passenger once put it nicely when I offered to trade seats so she could sit with her husband, "That's okay. We've been traveling together for a week. I'm tired of him."

Jerry announced that he wasn't traveling to every speech just to ask me leading questions. (Thank you, God.) But that conversation struck a chord. I started thinking, and by the time I had thunk out, it was all clear.

It Doesn't Change the Thermostat When I'm Not Looking

I didn't need anyone to travel with me and ask questions to prod my humor antenna. All I needed was a piece of paper with memory-jogging questions on it. If I had a sheet of paper with specific questions reminding me to look for humor, and if I filled out the sheet of paper on every trip, that would work just as well as taking someone along. (Plus, a sheet of paper won't adjust the thermostat when I'm not looking.) And if I fill out the sheet of paper in paragraph form rather than in list form, by the end of the year...wow!

That was the beginning of my system. In the next few days, I developed such a sheet of paper, a form of which has been with me to every speech since then. (Now it is in my note-book computer.) It requires a little discipline, but my journal has been a valuable tool that gathers not just ideas but also anecdotes written up and ready to use.

Best of all, funny stuff no longer gets away.

But the (Gulp) Name?

I can explain that. When I put together my first humor journal, I wasn't sure it would work for my own purposes, much less anyone else's. One day when my right brain was napping, my left brain reared its head and named the page "Jeanne's Journal System for Gathering Original, Nontopical, Humorous Speech Material."

This insufferable title was nicknamed "Jeanne's Journals." Give me a break on this if you're scoring on originality. Creativity wasn't my goal. I just needed something at the top of the pages so I wouldn't tell my secretary to run off the whatchamacallits or to pull the doowhichamaditties off the computer. So, Jeanne's Journals it became to me and soon, to my buddies in the National Speakers Association.

When I decided to put my system in writing, I started worrying that it needed a better title. Something zippy. Hot. Cutting edge. I mentioned this to my friend Norma, a teacher, and explained that in today's world, titles need to pop off the page.

Norma was honest. Jeanne's Journals was not cutting edge. She suggested…"Norma's Journals."

You get what you pay for.

Forget about popping off the page. For now I'll be explaining Jeanne's Journal System. In Part IV, you will learn how to develop your own journal. At that point, strike out my name and put in yours. That's what Norma would do.

The Advantages

Jeanne's Journal System offers several advantages:

- *Jeanne's Journal System leads you to look at the world through humorous eyes.* The effect of keeping a daily humor journal and making a concentrated effort to find stuff pushes you to look at the world through humorous eyes. The mere knowledge that the blank spaces on your humor journal will be staring you in the face every day takes your humor awareness to a higher level.

- *Jeanne's Journal System creates a collection of winners vs it'll-do's.* Most speakers and writers select the topic or message, develop the points, and then start looking for stories to illustrate them. While the stories are certainly important in these instances, they are not the priority. In the crunch to meet deadlines, we often settle for it'll-do's. Speeches, sermons, articles, and training sessions are full of it'll-do's because somebody couldn't find anything better.

- *Jeanne's Journal System leads you to work in reverse.* You gather terrific, life-experience stories with no specific idea of how you will use them. You look for them, find them, and store them away. Then, when you need relevant, personal examples, they are at your fingertips. People will rave about your illustrations, which won't be a surprise. That's why you collected the stories in the first place.

Jeanne's Journal System prepares you for the unexpected. With a supply of winners at your fingertips, you'll be quicker to accept invitations to speak or write. You may even seek opportunities because you know that an entire program or article can be built around a great story. (A speaker friend of mine says, "I speak from the heart. But it's amazing how heartfelt a message can become when first I have a good story to illustrate it.") In addition, reading through your supply of stories every so often makes you a better ad-libber.

Jeanne's Journal System produces written stories rather than lists of ideas. It encourages you to jot down, but only until you can write up. Lists of ideas are replaced by vignettes.

Jeanne's Journal System yields illustrations unique to you. Because your journal is personalized, you stock up on stories from your life experiences, not Winston Churchill's or Knute Rockne's. A story didn't have to happen to you, but it does mean you heard about it, saw it, or experienced it on the fringe. You can thus tell about it with a personal touch. Even if someone else takes your story (and survives being placed before a firing squad), he or she can't tell it from your vantage point.

Jeanne's Journal System turns a minimum investment of time into a wealth of material. This is an ongoing process, but it should not be time-consuming! Only a few minutes daily are needed to fill in a journal. If it takes an hour, reevaluate how you're going about it. Something's wrong. I make my living telling stories, and good material means my reputation. This system produces hundreds of vignettes a year for me, but I rarely spend even thirty minutes a day filling in my journal, and I never spend my most productive time on it. Of course, with practice you'll get faster. I've learned not to stare at the journal wondering how to write up a story. I just write it up in some form and move on.

- *Jeanne's Journal System lets you accumulate material when you are immersed in other projects.* That is what I meant by *Don't Let the Funny Stuff Get Away.* If great stories are happening around you on the days when you are especially creative or have lots of time to look for them, they're also happening on days when this is not the case. This system let's you plod right along gathering humor at times when you're immersed in other projects.

In addition to the advantages already outlined, this Jeanne's Journal System works especially well for professional speakers for a few additional reasons:

- Professional speakers have numerous humor-gathering opportunities. Unlike people who work in one environment with the same persons day after day, professional speakers move around and interact with large numbers of different people in a variety of situations.
- Professional speakers have a lot of slack time. These are periods when we feel as though we're wasting or losing precious time, and there is not one darned thing we can do about it. When we are at home or at the office and the exterminator is running late, we can always do something for a few minutes to be a little more productive.

It's not that easy when we are on the road. Examples of slack time for me are sitting in airport gate areas, riding in cabs, and waiting to get in a hotel room, to name a few. There is not enough time to jump into big projects.

At first glance, these occasions appear to be nonproductive, toe-tapping, and thumb-twiddling times. But they don't have to be. Through the years I have helped friends develop humor journals. Slack time is often missing for those friends who speak as an avocation rather than as a vocation. They have to set aside time to fill in their humor journals. Other forces often dictate when you will write up. You just take advantage of those occasions.

- *Professional speakers have an easy, natural way to group our humor journals, i.e., one journal per speech.* The big decision is when to fill in the spaces. Daily? Every two days? Weekly? For professional speakers, this is a simple, natural decision. One journal per speech. Each journal will include the humor ops at the actual presentation as well as the humor ops with travel, correspondence, lodging, people you meet on that trip, and so forth.

Chapter 10

DEVELOPING THE JOURNAL

When I began to develop my original humor journal, my first step was to identify the humor ops in my day. *Humor ops* are the places and occasions in my typical schedule where and when humor is most likely to happen.

At the time, I was traveling and speaking approximately twenty-three days each month for ten months of the year. On a typical day I left home or a hotel, went to the airport, traveled to another city and another hotel, spoke, and eventually headed out again—after a good night's sleep if I was lucky.

I went wild with my first step and listed over sixty opportunities that I thought would provide humor during a speaking trip. From flight attendants and pilots to waitresses and people in my audiences, I listed all of them. The simple, single sheet of memory joggers I envisioned was getting crowded.

Closer examination revealed that many of these items could be lumped together. For example, I could include items such as ticket agents, flight attendants and pilots under *Airlines*. Taxis, limos, shuttles, and rental car agencies fit under

Ground transportation. My second step, therefore, was to combine as many items as possible. This took my list from over sixty items down to fifteen.

After I narrowed my list to this smaller number, my third task was to arrange the items, as nearly as possible, according to their usual occurrence during my day. Like most people, my days are seldom identical; they generally they fall into similar patterns. Listing the items according to my most normal schedule was not a difficult task so long as I didn't become persnickety. My first humor ops come during my travel. The next humor ops involve my lodging, then my speech, and so forth.

A few leftover items couldn't be listed in chronological order. These were placed in a *Miscellaneous* category. For example, I call home or the office several times a day and am likely to hear something humorous, so I added a *Home* category and put it under *Miscellaneous*. In this step—arranging the items chronologically—I ended up with three main categories: *Travel*, *Booking*, and *Miscellaneous*. It is not necessary to have a few main categories. It simply worked that way for me.

Studying my items and the emerging journal at that point, I thought of a few categories that didn't fit into my routine day but would help me gather humor or be a better speaker. They would act as little assignments to myself. As long as I was going to fill in this sheet, why not use it to improve? An example is the category *New Material to Try*. I fill this category in before every speech. It makes me stretch.

My original long list of humor ops was now combined and arranged. The remaining step was to create the form.

I used a handwritten journal for the first eight years. It was one sheet, front and back. When I created that form, I left space between each item to write in what I found. Since the space was small, it made me think in terms of the short vignette. Small spaces didn't make the task seem overwhelming. Occasionally when there were longer stories, I continued them on additional pages, which I paper-clipped to the journal. In general, though, I tried to fit a story into the space provided.

I filled out my page by hand on trips and then gave it to my secretary to input into her computer…if she could read my writing. Because the page was arranged by categories, she did not have to make decisions as to where items should be filed in the computer. She simply stored them in the computer in big files named for the categories on the journal.

As with anything of this type, the page underwent slight revisions when I started using it regularly, but there have been few changes from the basic original journal. The only big change I have made is in record keeping.

The form is now in my laptop computer, and I type in the stories as I find them. The form (the old sheet) is stored in a key file. I simply pull that key into a new file and make a new journal for each trip. The amount of space between categories is no longer relevant because as I type, of course, the headings move down. This has cut out a time-consuming step for my secretary. Now her main responsibilities are to pull out the stories at the end of the year, stack them up, and laugh. She is happy.

Following is the journal that goes with me on each trip.

Jeanne's Journal
(Front)

Booking # _____ Client: _____

Date: _____ Contact: _____

Location: _____

Travel

Airlines:

People:

Ground Transportation:

Lodging:

Dining:

AOC:

Booking

Correspondence:

New Material to Try:

Speech Setup:

Speech Intro:

Jeanne's Journal
(Back)

Audience:

New Material Tried:

Most Memorable Occurrence:

Speaking Tips:

Miscellaneous

Tried in Conversation:

Trip Funny:

Speakers:

Home:

Ideas to Write Up:

Catchall:

Explanation of Categories
Jeanne's Journal
Travel

Airlines:

Includes airline and airport personnel—flight attendants, pilots, club room hosts, counter and gate agents, bag checkers, "red coats," cleaning crews, security screeners.

People:

Includes anybody you come in contact with while traveling—passengers, people sending off or greeting other passengers.

Ground Transportation:

Includes cabs, shuttles, rental cars, MARTA, limos, drivers, clients meeting you. However you get from the airport to your ground destination comes under this category. Since this sheet is being filled in by the trip, also fill in this category on the return. If you drive to the speech, material found during that time goes here (convenience stores, gas stations, flea markets on the way, etc.).

Lodging:

Where you stay in connection with a speech—bellhop, parking garage, check-in people, housekeeping, telephone operators, maintenance, etc.

Dining:

Room service people, menus, wait staff, people around you in restaurants, hosts.

AOC (area of the country):

Humor that is related to locale. For one thing, you get good stories. For another, you can use the stories when you return to the same area. Over the course of time, you'll have material for every AOC and many cities.

Booking

Correspondence:
Anything humorous in connection with correspondence/calls with this particular client. I usually check correspondence and review calls while traveling to the trip so it fits here.

New Material to Try:
This is not for adding new stories. It is here to encourage using new material. Filling in this category before each speech nudges me toward trying something new. It makes me plan ahead. Later, seeing what I had intended to do, makes me accountable to myself. (If journal is handwritten, leave a small space.)

Speech Setup:
Anything amusing or unbelievable about the way the room is set for the program.

Speech Intro:
We send a prepared introduction, but many introducers spruce it up and show their creativity. It becomes a story.

Audience:
Anything humorous or bizarre, said/done by *any* audience member before/during/after speech. Includes emcee, head table folks, award recipients, door prize committee and winners, etc.

New Material Tried:
Follow-up category for the one on the front. Jot down any new pieces of material you try in the speech, including ad-libs.

Most Memorable Occurrence:

The most memorable thing about the speech. I think *humor* here, but this could also be the place for those true, moving stories that happen. Don't start keeping a diary. Think vignette. Think illustration. If nothing comes to mind, skip it.

Speaking Tips:

What is learned. Category for future speeches or articles. Mistakes made, something learned from this speech. Tweak it with humor.

Miscellaneous

Tried in Conversation:

This is an important jotting down place. Moving a story from the journal to a speech starts right here. *After* you obtain a story but *before* you use it in a speech, try it in conversation and note that on your journal. Keeps stories moving toward perfection.

Trip Funny:

The old goal—one funny thing a day—is now this section. Include odd little stories or quotes from newspapers, jokes told during event, signs spotted, generic stuff, any items that strike you funny, fit with your style—and do not come from another speaker's material.

Speakers:

Include business associates, which for me would be other speakers. Include personal interaction stories about every speaker you have contact with during this trip. (The time will come when you have to introduce them.)

Home:

Include family, friends, business here as well as material resulting from calls and e-mails home.

Ideas to Write Up:

This is the place to jot down ideas and events to write up or just think about. List longer story ideas that pop into memory during this trip and stories to develop when you have more time. Turn to this category first when you have spare time to write up.

Catchall:

The journal process is not the goal. There are no grades for perfect journals. Jeanne's Journal System is a tool to get the final product—personal stories. Don't waste time trying to fit stories into the right cubbyholes. Confused about where to put a story? Throw it in here and move on.

Chapter 11

STORIES FROM ONE SPEAKER'S JOURNAL

Here are stories that came straight off my journal. I've shown them in the journal category where they were placed. I found them by obeying the LAWS outlined in Part II.

❂ ❂ ❂

Travel—Airlines

"War Eagle," the flight attendant said when I handed her my ticket at the boarding area. She had noticed my Auburn University hanging bag, which is precisely why I carry it around the country. It's a great way to meet other Auburn folks like her, and usually they greet me as she did: "War Eagle."

I was one of the last passengers to board. After we chatted briefly, she followed me down the jetway. The minute I walked around the galley of the plane, the comments started.

"Oh, no! An Auburn fan!" a man in the first row said with a big grin. Seven other men in the rows near him chimed in.

"They're letting anybody fly these days, even War Eagles."
"Surely she's not sitting up here." I was. I had a bump-up
coupon like the rest of them. The flight attendant said nothing.
I had run smack-dab into a bunch of University of Alabama
guys on a golfing trip. I quipped something like, "Did one of
you remember to bring the club and ball?"

The good-natured comments continued as I found a place
for my carry-on luggage and made a big deal out of hanging the
Auburn bag in the front of the closet, "so you can see it first
when the doors are opened." Their booing drowned out the
sound of my voice.

The flight attendant said nothing—until she came from
the galley a few minutes later with a small piece of paper in
hand. "Okay," she announced in a loud voice, "a first-class section of Alabama fans. What kind of *cheap beer* do you guys
want?"

✪ ✪ ✪

People

The nonstop flight from Atlanta to Honolulu is almost nine
hours, which is long for adults and a lifetime for children.
Thankfully, we were in first class because of coupons. A nine-
year-old girl and a seven-year-old boy sat in the center seats
across from us.

Their parents had the two seats on the other side and held
their third child, a baby girl whose only seat was on someone's
lap. The "someone" changed constantly. For eight hours the
family squirmed, played games, mumbled at one another, and
jostled the baby, who never slept despite the fact that her mom
had given her a big spoonful of cough syrup right before we
lifted off. Six hours into the flight, I wanted to ask for the rest
of the syrup for myself.

The flight was a constant fruit basket turnover that meant every member of the family sat in every seat at some point and took turns trying to placate the baby.

As we approached our destination, the flight attendant asked the seven-year-old boy if it was his first trip to Hawaii. He said, "No, ma'am, it's my second trip. And it's my Daddy's *last* trip."

❀ ❀ ❀

Ground Transportation

In the mid-eighties I flew into New Orleans, and two women officials of the group I was to address met me. On the way into town, they discussed the ongoing poor performance of the New Orleans Saints.

Said one, "If the Saints ever have a winning season, people around here won't know how to act. They've followed the team for years even though it doesn't win." She shook her head back and forth. "I don't understand it. Can you imagine sticking with a loser for seventeen years?"

The other woman, recently divorced, quipped, "Well, I stuck with one for over thirty."

❀ ❀ ❀

Lodging

A family got on an elevator with me in Oregon, and I asked the towel-wrapped little boy if he had been swimming. "Yes, ma'am," he drawled, sounding familiarly southern.

Way up there in the Great Northwest, I couldn't resist asking my next question. "Well, where is your accent from?"

He dug a toe into the carpet and said shyly, "It's from North Carolina."

"It is?"

"Yes, ma'am. And I am too."

❁ ❁ ❁

Dining

Five minutes after ordering a cheeseburger and baked potato through room service at a hotel in Duncan, Oklahoma, I called back to request that Heinz 57 sauce, mustard, mayo, butter, salt, and pepper be added to my order. Within minutes, there was a knock on the door and a young woman from the restaurant thrust a bottle of Heinz 57 in my direction. Then she reached in the pockets on her smock and pulled out an assortment of little packages. "Here's the rest of the stuff."

I took all the condiments and said, "This is great, but I don't have the cheeseburger yet."

She said, "I know it. But we're real busy, and I'm just filling what orders we can."

❁ ❁ ❁

I checked into the hotel in Casper, Wyoming, after a long trip, and immediately called room service. It was the middle of the afternoon, and I was afraid the restaurant was closed. A young-sounding male voice answered. "Do you have baked potatoes this time of the day?" I inquired, figuring like most places they did not. He said, "Not usually, but I'm the executive chef. I can get you a baked potato if you want it."

Within thirty minutes the chef, who couldn't have been much older than twenty, delivered my order. "How does one get to be an executive chef at your age?" I asked.

"You get to be executive chef," he explained, putting down my tray, "when three people don't show up for work."

❀ ❀ ❀

AOC

I gazed upward in amazement at the nine clocks behind the registration desk at the Sheraton in Washington, D.C. Each clock gave the time from a different spot around the world, and, of course, the hour hands varied with the time zones. You would expect that the minute hands would be on the identical minute on all of the clocks. They weren't. So I pointed to the clocks and said to the desk clerk, "What's the deal here with your clocks? I don't believe they're working properly."

He didn't even glance backwards when he said, "The deal is, you're in Washington, D.C. Everything's screwed up here."

❀ ❀ ❀

Holland, Michigan, is one of the most Republican counties in the United States, and President Bush had campaigned there the day before my Chamber of Commerce speech in '92. The town was still abuzz when I arrived. During the reception before the banquet—which was jokingly called a "Republican caucus"—all the talk was about the election, President Bush, and Republican politics. Everyone made it a point to say, "You may not be aware of it, but this is the strongest Republican county in the country."

When I moved away from one small group of people at the reception, a woman tugged on my sleeve. Feeling compelled to let the out-of-towner know a little more, she whispered, "Everybody here is not a Republican."

I whispered back, "They told me there was one of you."

Horrified, she asked, "Did someone say something about me?"

I teased, "Sure. They see your vote every time. There is always one, and they know whose it is."

During table conversation later, I related the incident, which I thought was humorous, but was met with blank stares for several seconds.

Finally, one man squinted his eyes and broke the silence. "Exactly what did the woman look like?"

❀ ❀ ❀

Booking–Correspondence

A letter received from a 1997 client with information about the company had this notation: "This will give some background on our company, but keep in mind this was written in 1980."

❀ ❀ ❀

Before each speech, we send the client an information sheet that outlines the details of my travel. If the client indicates that someone will meet my plane, the next question is, "Please describe the individual who will be meeting Jeanne."

A secretary wrote: "My boss will meet Jeanne at the airport. If I describe him, I will lose my job."

❀ ❀ ❀

Speech Setup

I put on my warm-up outfit the afternoon of a banquet in Minneapolis and went to check the meeting room before heading out to walk. The huge facility was empty, and I had a question about the setup. Someone in the kitchen told me to wait in the ballroom while he contacted the person in charge.

Back in the large hall, I passed the time counting tables, checking silverware, and straightening centerpieces. Not in a speaker's normal contract, but what the heck? It seemed like the neighborly thing.

Unbeknownst to me, I had a couple of companions. Two guys working on the spotlights were behind a one-way glass up in the audiovisual room at the back of the hall, and they had me under constant surveillance.

Minutes ticked away, and I was getting antsy because my exercise time was dwindling. I started stretching a little, reaching for my toes if not actually touching them every time. Still no one came.

In a few more minutes, I moved out of sight of the main doors, got on the floor, and started doing sit-ups. Up, down, up, down. I hit my limit quickly, struggling on the last ones—thirty-eeeeight, thirt-tee-ninnnne, forty!—and fell back onto the floor in exhaustion.

Suddenly, a spotlight clicked its full beam directly on my sprawled body. A voice boomed through the sound system, "Come on, ma'am. You can do five more."

❂ ❂ ❂

Speech Intro

I'm assuming he didn't realize what he said, but one never knows. The introducer said: "Our speaker tonight is Jeanne Robertson, who used to be a beauty."

❂ ❂ ❂

After years of being introduced as everything from a former Miss North America to a lady who tries to be funny, we started sending a short, to-the-point introduction to each client. It is double-spaced in extra large print for easy reading. Occasionally, however, introducers will attempt to work from memory and mess up. Quite often they go blank right after "Our speaker today is..."

When this happens, I usually chime in, very deliberately, with "Jean-ne Rob-ert-son." It always gets a laugh. Through the years I have occasionally even handed my name badge or place card to the introducer for a second laugh.

My favorite comeback to this was from an introducer who read my place card and then turned back toward me to ask, "And just how do we know you are seated in the right place?"

✿ ✿ ✿

Okay, perhaps there was a slight age difference.

My introducer at one speech said, "I grew up in the Tarheel State and remember seeing our speaker on TV when she was Miss North Carolina. I said, "Look, Mommy!"

✿ ✿ ✿

Introduced by a University of Alabama fan who said: "Jeanne decided not to pursue a formal education. She's a 1967 graduate of Auburn University."

✿ ✿ ✿

Audience

A woman told me her sixteen-year-old son sailed through the written part of his driver's license exam and gave the waiting father a smug thumbs-up. Then he sat down to get his eyes examined and put his right hand over his right eye. The patrolman said, "No, both eyes," and the kid covered up his other eye with his left hand.

❂ ❂ ❂

When I spoke at a national convention in Texas during the summer of '94, it had been just three weeks since there had been bad floods in Georgia. I was surprised, therefore, when the woman seated beside me said she was from the flooded area. She told me how horrible it had been and added, "It's been three weeks, and we don't have our water back yet."

"And you came to the convention?" I asked.

"My husband wanted me to come," she assured me. "He said he was tired of toting water for two people."

❂ ❂ ❂

Most Memorable Occurrence

A group invited me back to speak after a twenty-year lapse, and we sent my current publicity information and latest photo. Therefore, I was a little surprised to arrive at the registration area and see a twenty-year-old, blown-up picture of me on an easel outside the banquet room. I was staring at the poster when a man walked up and started staring with me. After a few moments he asked, "Is that you?"

I was still so amazed at seeing this picture again in my lifetime that it took a few seconds to respond. Eventually I managed to mumble, "Well, I guess so."

More silence.

Finally, he turned and said, "What happened?"

❂ ❂ ❂

Speaking Tips

I didn't see a microphone when I arrived in Camden, South Carolina, to speak to a fairly good-size dinner club. The event was being held in a restaurant, and the main room jutted off in several directions. People who couldn't drag their chairs into the main room would be out of sight of the speaker. A sound system would help the situation, but one wasn't set up. I hesitantly asked my contact if he had received our letter about needing a microphone.

"Yes." Silence.

I was almost scared to ask. "Were...were you able to get a microphone?"

He folded his arms and replied proudly, "Anybody good enough to speak to the Camden Dinner Club is good enough to speak without a microphone."

Speaking tip: Learn to shout!

Trip Funny

Obituary section: Rather than attend his annual board meeting, the company treasurer took a room at a Motel 6 not far from his home, and stabbed himself to death with a kitchen knife. A company executive said, "This was totally unlike him. It was something he had never done before."

A man bought his first computer and bargained for a thirty-day trial period. If it didn't work out, he could return it in a month. After fifteen days, he called the company and asked two things: (1) Did he have to keep it for thirty days? and (2) Did he have to return it in one piece?

❂ ❂ ❂

Speakers

The renowned insurance consultant's remarks were over, and it was time for questions from the good ole boys in the company. After a few awkward seconds of silence, a fellow rose. "Some companies are getting into personal lines, and some companies are getting out. Is it that some companies are dumber than others? If so, are the dumb ones getting in or out?"

The high-priced consultant answered, "Yes."

❂ ❂ ❂

I have introduced myself to Mississippi humorist Jerry Clower a number of times in airports through the years. By this point Jerry knows he's met me several times, but he always has a little trouble placing where or when. He covers well, but it's apparent to me he is lost at placing exactly why I seem familiar.

Once in the Atlanta Airport I saw him entertaining a crowd of travelers who had gathered around, so I ambled over to wait my turn and introduce myself again. We work a lot of the same meetings, I explained, and we had chatted on several occasions. Oh, yes. He remembered me, he proclaimed. But I had my doubts.

Anyway, the pleasantries continued, and I asked how he was getting along. Suddenly, we were good friends. He said, "Oh Jeanne, I'm so tired. If I could just travel around and have some time to myself, but I can't do that. You see how the crowds gather. People recognize me and come up all the time. I'm not going to be rude, so I always talk. But I am worn out. I wish I could just travel incognito."

I glanced down. Written in huge letters on the side of his suitcase: JERRY CLOWER.

❂ ❂ ❂

Home

My sixty-year-old, white-haired husband forced himself into a lingerie section of a local department store to buy me a birthday present and was taken aback by some of the styles. An eager young salesclerk, trying to be helpful, held up a particularly skimpy, sexy little number and asked, "Would your wife like to sleep in that?"

Jerry replied, "She might, if she could still wear her socks."

❂ ❂ ❂

After traveling all week I arrived at the hotel in Indianapolis around 7:00 P.M. and immediately checked with Jerry back home when I got to my room. Most of the conversation consisted of me telling him how tired I was and how I really needed a good night's sleep. My speech was early the next morning, and I was heading straight to bed. I was worn out. Completely whipped to a frazzle.

When I hung up, I noticed from information on the bedside table that the new Circle Mall had opened in Indianapolis. It was accessible to my hotel through a walkway, and it had a Nordstrom—my favorite place to shop. The word *Nordstrom* always perks me up. It's a family quirk.

When I returned home the next night, Jerry immediately asked how the speeches had gone, and I told him. Had I been able to get a good night's sleep Friday, he wanted to know. He had been concerned that I was so tired.

"Oh, yes," I assured him, not mentioning the trip to Nordstrom. "I felt much better by morning. I just needed to crash."

"But you were able to get to bed early?" he questioned again.

"Yes," I lied, for no reason other than it seemed like the thing to do.

Jerry got that little smiley smirk on his face that husbands can get and handed me a piece of paper. "Well, here. You'd better call this number and talk to the people at Visa. Someone charged $332.47 to your card at Nordstrom around 9:00 o'clock last night in Indianapolis. Wonder who it was?"

At 11:00 o'clock the night before, Jerry had been awakened by a call from someone at Visa headquarters. Their computers had kicked out a red flag on my card because charges were being placed on the same card from three locations at approximately the same time. First, someone at Global Travel in Burlington had charged tickets on my card late that afternoon. Jerry explained that could certainly be possible. His wife's airline tickets were always charged to her Visa card.

Someone else had been charging on that same card number at the same time in Florida, the Visa representative told him. That could be possible too, Jerry explained. His wife's secretary was in Florida on vacation but was keeping up with business via long distance. She easily could have ordered something for the office late that afternoon and put it on that card.

Then the woman wanted to know if someone could have charged $332.47 to that identical card earlier that evening at Nordstrom in Indianapolis. "That's when I became concerned," Jerry told me with a fake puzzled look. "I told her that my wife was in Indianapolis, but it could not have been her. I had talked to her earlier and she was going straight to bed. She was absolutely worn out."

I said, "You were correct, but I took a drink of Nordstrom and felt much better."

❀ ❀ ❀

For a man with a doctoral degree, my husband is sometimes clueless.

Right after our son, Beaver, graduated from high school, he had a date with a girl at college in a nearby town. Since he had a poor driving record and would be on a busy highway, I remarked to Jerry that I hated for Beaver to be on the interstate so late at night.

Jerry, high school class of 1955 and sometime still thinking in that era, said, "Well, he won't be too late. Won't she have to be in the dormitory around 9:00 on a weeknight?"

Ideas to Write Up
Comment by man as we went through convention buffet line: I was in the U.S. Army, and I've never seen food like this.

Part IV

DEVELOPING YOUR HUMOR JOURNAL

Chapter 12

GETTING STARTED

Now that you've seen my humor journal, it's time to get started on yours. If you are a professional speaker who travels often, you should be able to get off to a running start. You may be able to use Jeanne's Journal either verbatim or with minor changes, and you will have the advantages of a system that has been used for years.

My journal has provided not only an excellent system for collecting humor but also an organized, funny, written account of my career and valuable information for return speaking engagements. If your lifestyle is similar to mine, take my journal and let the fun begin. If your lifestyle does not involve speaking and traveling, you will need to develop your own journal. To do that, use the same steps I used to develop the original Jeanne's Journal. These are the four steps:

1. List your daily humor-gathering opportunities.
2. Combine list items into larger categories.
3. List categories in chronological order of your day.
4. Create the form.

Creating a Humor Journal Step-by-Step

To illustrate the step-by-step development of a humor journal, I am going to use my in-town journal. (Yes, I have one.) After obtaining good results from the original Jeanne's Journal for several years, I realized I was still letting a lot of funny stuff get away. The reason? I only filled in my journal when I was on the road giving speeches. Typically, these were periods when I had numerous humor-gathering opportunities and an abundance of slack time.

Would a system like this work, I wondered, if a person didn't have these two advantages? What if a person were in the same office every day, for example, with limited slack time?

To keep the funny stuff from getting away when I was at home, I drew up a journal that fit with my schedule when I was not traveling. I called it my in-town journal. Creating the format proved to be easy. I followed the same steps I used to develop the first journal. The challenge came in setting aside time to fill it in.

We will first go through the step-by-step process of developing a humor journal, using my in-town journal as an example. I'll address the time issue later.

Step 1—List Your Daily Humor-Gathering Opportunities

Humor ops are places or times you will most likely have opportunities to get stories. These are the occasions when you want to make sure to use the LAWS. Here are the twenty-five humor ops I listed for my typical in-town day:

Alterations
Answering machine messages
Cleaners
Computer guru

Conversations/visits with friends
Delivery people
Dinner
Drugstore
E-mail
Faxes
Grocery store
Local printer
Lunch
Meetings
Office supply store
Reports from humor buddies
Secretary
Snail mail
Social events
Son, daughter-in-law, grandchild, other relatives
Speakers
Sporting events
Spouse
Telephone conversations
Travel agency

Step 2—Combine List Items into Larger Categories

Look at your list of humor-gathering opportunities and see if you can lump any of them together. For example on my list, *snail mail*, *e-mail*, and *faxes* can be lumped together under *Mail*. Contact with my *travel agency*, *office supply store*, *local printer*, *computer guru*, and *delivery people* can be combined under *Business Associates*. Trips to the *grocery store*, *drugstore*, *cleaners*, and *alterations* can be lumped under *Errands*.

This step cut my list from twenty-five items down to eleven, a much more manageable amount. Here is the way I combined the categories:

Business associates Local printer, travel agency, office supply store, computer guru, delivery people
Errands Grocery store, cleaners, drugstore, alterations
Family Spouse, son, daughter-in-law, grandchild, other relatives
Friends Conversations/visits with friends, reports from humor buddies
Mail snail mail, e-mail, faxes
Meals Lunch, dinner, all of them (we eat out often, many humor ops)
Meetings
Phone Telephone conversations, answering machine messages
Secretary
Speakers
Special events Sporting events, social events

You may have categories that fit best under *Miscellaneous*. As with the original Jeanne's Journal, there were several categories that I wanted to add to my in-town journal to encourage me to improve. They have been explained on pages 88 and 94 and are *Tried in conversation, Daily funny (Trip funny), Ideas to write up,* and *Catchall*.

Step 3—List Categories in Chronological Order of Your Day

     Secretary
     Phone
     Mail

Business Associates
Meetings
Meals
Errands
Family
Humor Buddies/Friends
Special Events
Speakers

Step 4—Create the Form

The items listed in the last step now go on a form that can be handwritten or input into a computer. For the handwritten version, list the items but leave spaces in which to write. Run off copies of the handwritten version, using front and back of a single sheet of paper. For the computer version, the form becomes a standard file you pull up and fill in. My form for this journal is on the next page. My in-town journal is always in my computer. This is the starter page/file. Space between categories is not necessary when working on a computer because as you type, the categories move down.

And, folks, that's it! Now it's time to use the LAWS and start filling in the journal spaces.

Jeanne's In-Town Journal

Date:

Secretary:

Phone:

Mail:

Business Associates:

Meetings:

Meals:

Errands:

Family:

Humor Buddies/Friends:

Special Events:

Speakers:

Tried in Conversation:

Daily Funny:

Ideas to Write Up:

Catchall:

Chapter 13

STORIES FROM AN IN-TOWN JOURNAL

Just for the fun of it, here are some stories that came right off the in-town journal we've used as a guide in this section.

Secretary

Before I spoke to the Women's Club in Wheeling, West Virginia, I called my contact and asked if a friend from that area could accompany me. She agreed, and was thrilled to learn that the friend I referred to was former Miss America, Jacquelyn Mayer Townsend.

Six years later I scheduled a return engagement with the same club. When we booked it, my secretary, Toni, remembered a woman who had called the office months earlier. She had read my book and wanted us to let her know when I spoke in her area. She lived near Wheeling. Because she was a friend of a friend, we called the club hostess to ask if I could bring a guest. Quite frankly, this was all a little unusual, and I had forgotten I had made the same unusual request of this group six years earlier.

My client was thrilled! "Oh, yes! The last time you brought a former Miss America. Who are you going to surprise us with this time?"

Toni called the guest to tell her it was all set up. Naturally, the woman asked what she should wear. Toni thought a second and said, "My only advice is to look the best you can, and bring a crown if you have one."

Phone

A client made a big deal to me in our pre-meeting telephone call over the fact that they never change a thing at their convention. Not a thing. They use the same format every year, even down to the meal menus. "We figure when it comes to the convention, if it ain't broke, don't fix it," he bragged. "It makes things easier on the committee."

I asked who had spoken at the banquet the year before, and he said, "It's our first year to have a speaker."

❁ ❁ ❁

Mail

Letter from a client about an upcoming speech—

> You will have a little more time on the program. The mayor had scheduled to be with us but had a prior commitment.

Now, let me think about that. If he had a prior commitment, why did he schedule to...

I had my opening line.

❁ ❁ ❁

After the question "How did you select your speaker?" one client scribbled in, "Lottery."

❁ ❁ ❁

In a letter received from a client for an upcoming speech: "Our teenage daughter will be away for the weekend, and we would like for Jeanne to stay with us and sleep in her room. I assure you, Jeanne will have a quiet, peaceful stay in that room, for I have noticed my daughter never seems to hear me, even when I raise my voice to a healthy scream."

❁ ❁ ❁

Business Associates

Hi-tech doesn't eliminate small-town gossip. It enhances it.

My secretary, Toni, bounded into the office early one Monday morning and wanted to know how long I planned to be on a diet.

What in the world? How did she know I was dieting?

Sandra, down at Global Travel told her, she explained.

"Sandra? At Global Travel?"

"Yep. Delta Air Lines told Sandra."

Delta Air Lines tells my travel agent who tells my secretary that I am on a diet? And how did they know?

There is always an explanation. Toni had whipped by Global Travel that morning to pick up a ticket. When Sandra pulled up my record in the computer, she saw that the night before I had changed all my airline meals for that week to salads, and figured it was because I was dieting. She told my secretary. My secretary asked me.

Everybody was right. I'm dieting. I'm dieting! Put it on the World Wide Web!

❁ ❁ ❁

Meetings

At an Arts Council meeting in my hometown, we were discussing how much it would cost to have a float in the upcoming Christmas parade.

One of my friends, looking at the parade information, said, "Oh, look. We don't have to pay. Jeanne, you can ride for us for free. It says 'there will be no charge for beauty queens and cars over thirty-five years old.' "

❁ ❁ ❁

Meals

My husband, Jerry, is a kind, loving, nice man, but he is known for being tight with the dollar. Although from time to time he protests the label, his actions give him away.

Several couples went to dinner at Sidetracks, a local restaurant that puts the specials of the day on a blackboard near the cash register.

After we looked at the menus, someone in our party asked if anyone could see well enough to see the specials. Jerry said he could see distances and squinted his eyes and started reading aloud: "Six ninety-five, ten ninety-five, eight ninety-five, and four ninety-five."

Then he advised, "I think the last one sounds the best."

❁ ❁ ❁

Errands

I went to my local grocery store in North Carolina on a Fall Saturday afternoon. Since it was football season, I had on my Auburn sweatshirt even though the school is located several states away in Alabama. Imagine my surprise to see a guy wearing a sweatshirt of Auburn's number-one rival, the University of Alabama, pushing a cart right in my direction. We both stopped in our tracks to talk about the upcoming game between the two schools.

Minutes later he said that he was no longer a big Bama football fan. What was this? An Alabama guy who wasn't a big football fan? It seemed like an oxymoron. I didn't know this was possible and couldn't wait to tell about it the next time I spoke in Auburn. Needing a little more information, I asked him, "What happened?"

He drawled, "Well, to tell you the truth, when Bear Bryant died, and three days later he didn't rise up, it shook my faith."

✪ ✪ ✪

She was about my age, so I found it was easy to identify with her.

I watched with amusement as a lady went from cart to cart trying to find her groceries in the local grocery store. When she thought she had located it, another woman stepped forward and said, "This is mine. I think that's yours," and she pointed to an unattended basket.

The first woman said, "I looked at that one, but I didn't remember buying crackers. Oh, well," she shrugged, and then broke into a big smile. "I'm out of crackers, so I'll take it."

And she wheeled the cart away.

✪ ✪ ✪

Family

My Aunt Carolyn had hired a moving company to help get a bunch of stuff to their house when they closed the family drugstore in Auburn, Alabama. The largest item to be moved was the soda fountain, which she intended to use in her game room.

When the driver arrived he immediately zeroed in on the massive fountain and asked, "Does that go?" She told him it did, and without missing a beat he said, "We'll get it Monday."

"Do you have a special piece of equipment for heavy things coming in Monday?" Carolyn inquired.

He drawled, "No, ma'am. Monday I'll be on vacation in Tennessee."

❂ ❂ ❂

Humor Buddies/Friends

Friends Pat and Buell Moser heard that I had spoken in Lawton, Oklahoma, and told me they lived there as newlyweds. They rented a tiny house that had one big room with a little kitchen and bath. The big room was the bedroom at night, the living room during the day, and the dining room at mealtime.

Pat said her parents and brothers returned home after a visit and told everyone that "Pat and Buell have a television in *every* room."

❂ ❂ ❂

One of my humor scouts, Wesley Ellis, told me about an acquaintance named Pearl Jean who was an active member of her church choir. As the Christmas holidays approached, she desperately wanted the group to perform at the prison where her brother was the warden. She extolled the group's hard work and accomplishments to her sibling. Wouldn't it be wonderful for the inmates to benefit from the joyous sounds of her friends from the church?

The warden listened to his sister's offer and slowly shook his head. He didn't think it was a good idea.

"And why not?" she persisted.

"Because," he answered, "some of the prisoners might not be guilty."

❄ ❄ ❄

Special Events

My husband and I were sitting in the stands during an Elon College football game when a voice over the loud speaker got everyone's attention during halftime. It was time to announce the Queen of the Game!

My good friend Norma, also the Elon athletic director's wife, leaned over to tell me this was something that would happen at every game that year. A local florist donated flowers, which would be brought to the Queen by a student.

By then the announcer was saying that the Queen of the Game was in such and such section. It was ours. I had a sinking feeling in my stomach.

Sure enough, seconds later the voice boomed, "And our Queen of the Game is...Jeanne Robertson!" Everyone around me laughed. When the flowers arrived seconds later, I stood and waved and blew kisses.

When the game was over, the athletic director, Dr. Alan White, came over to where we were still talking. I, of course, was still holding the large bouquet of flowers. "Okay, Alan," I began. "Where are my prizes? Do I get a scholarship?"

A sly, fund-raising smile crept across his face. "No, Jeanne. You don't understand. The Queen of the Game isn't someone who *receives* a scholarship. The Queen of the Game is someone we think might *give* a scholarship."

❄ ❄ ❄

Speakers

Mike McKinney, who runs the Carl Hurley Cavalcade of Comedy, among other things, was visiting in our home and told us about his wonderful cabin on a lake in Kentucky. He said,

"Everybody has a deck. At 3:00 o'clock, we sit around on our decks and decide which deck we're gonna be on at 5:00 o'clock."

❁ ❁ ❁

Humorist and fiddle player Doc Blakely from Wharton, Texas, is known for his quick wit. One Sunday afternoon I received a call from him. Before we hung up, he said, "Are you busy this week?" Speakers like to know if other speakers are busy.

I told him that I was and added, "This afternoon, I spoke to the VIPs of Alamance County, and I head out of town in the morning. You gonna be busy, Doc?" Notice the way I brushed over *VIPs*. I knew that would get his attention. I could practically see him mulling over what I said.

"Yes, I'll be out of town several days." He paused. "The VIPs?" he repeated. "On Sunday afternoon? That's a little unusual. What was that group?"

"The V-I-Ps," I responded slowly, and then quickly changed the subject. "Tell Pat hello for me."

"Sure, I'll tell her. Say, I don't believe I've ever heard of the VIPs. Who are they?"

Enough was enough. "The VIPs are the Visually Impaired Persons of my county," I admitted.

Doc said, "Aha! Now there's a group you'll be able to convince that you were in the Miss America Pageant!"

❁ ❁ ❁

North Carolina's longtime Commissioner of Agriculture, Jim Graham, strode to the front of the picnic area to address the members of the North Carolina LP Gas Association at their annual convention. There was no lectern for notes, but the commissioner did not need one. He had a small piece of paper curled in his left hand, but without looking at it, he began his "few words" to the audience. A politician reminiscent of tent revival days, he was accustomed to being before an audience. It comes with being commissioner of agriculture over thirty years. Heaven only knows how many pickin's he has pulled off a pig and chickens he has eaten with his fingers.

The Commissioner grabbed the microphone in his right hand, planted his feet squarely on the ground, and slid his speech out of his mouth in good ole boy, Tarheel style. For the next few minutes he worked his crowd, the rolled piece of paper always prominent in his free hand. He combined the right amount of homespun humor and information about his department. People liked him. He was our kind of folk.

I was at the convention as a spouse but was watching through the eyes of a professional speaker. And as a professional speaker, there was no doubt in my mind as to what was written on that little piece of rolled up paper clutched in his fist. I waited to see how he pulled it off.

For a good twenty minutes, the commissioner spoke without missing a beat. But as he drew to a close, he drawled, "Wellllll," and at the same instant, slowly began unrolling the paper while continuing to look right in our eyes. "It's been my pleasure to be here," he continued. Then, *right then*, he sneaked a peek at the unrolled paper and read, "at the North Carolina LP Gas Association Convention." He looked up, smiled as his hands rolled the paper back up, and said, "Thank y'all for invitin' me."

❊ ❊ ❊

Daily Funny

Question: What's the difference between Alabama fans (or any school/politician that has lost a big game/race) and a litter of puppies?

Answer: In about four or five weeks, the puppies stop whining.

✿ ✿ ✿

Do you know how (any losing team) fans teach their children to count? 0-1, 0-2, 0-3.

✿ ✿ ✿

Letter to the editor in a Tennessee paper from a man concerned about cloning. He thought there ought to be a law against it, and I quote: "You let them have that cloning and before you know it, there'll be more Republicans."

✿ ✿ ✿

Ideas to Write Up
Line overheard: He could be a regular on Club Dance, but he would be one of those people sitting off to the side.

Chapter 14

A HUMOR JOURNAL EXPERIMENT

Through the years, I've explained my system for gathering humor to hundreds of professional speakers at chapter meetings of the National Speakers Association. As far back as 1985, NSA put one of those programs on a cassette that was sent to all twenty-five hundred members.

To test my system further for this book, I asked thirteen people to try a variation of the Jeanne's Journal System. They were selected because of their need for speech material, some needs greater than others. Also, these people lived in my vicinity and were willing to give this a try.

Among the people in the experimental group were

Two professional speakers
Two members of Toastmasters International
Two college administrators
A college coach
A training director

Two aspiring writers
Two business people
A minister
A high school teacher

After interviewing each of these individuals regarding his or her daily routine, I followed the four steps explained in the last section and customized a journal page for each person. The group came together, listened to an explanation of using the LAWS for finding humorous material, and headed out with their journals.

I later met with each one to learn the results. Their thoughts about the strengths and weaknesses of the process will help you develop your humor journal:

- *This journal system will work...if you need it.* The participants agreed that this type of journal system will certainly work but probably should be undertaken only by disciplined people who really need a large number of stories. They agreed it would take minimal time once you got in the flow of keeping the journal.
- *The journal system will make you humor aware.* All the participants agreed that their awareness of finding humor from their everyday experiences had been greatly increased from attempting to fill in a humor journal. Among those who said they did not need enough humorous material to warrant keeping a journal of this type on a regular basis, several stated that they were looking at the world through more humorous eyes.
- *The LAWS are great.* The information about looking, listening, and asking for humor turned the participants' antennae outward. Humor was indeed happening around them every day, and, in general, they found the LAWS section to be valuable. Even though all of the participants

give presentations of some type, most of them commented that they had never before thought about asking someone to tell them a funny story.

- *Some personal journal sheets needed adjustments.* Several participants made slight adjustments to the journal format that I had prepared for them. This is a natural part of the process. Through the years, my journal format has changed several times. My advice would be to plan to evaluate your format and make changes when necessary, adding or dropping categories.

  Be aware that your journal will vary with the time-consuming events in your life. When I took time to be in a play, I added the category *Play* and gathered material during rehearsals and performances.

  A third-grade class asked me to carry a stuffed animal (a travel buddy) with me for four months and write letters from everywhere we went. The little animal's name was *Lizzie*, and I added a *Lizzie* category during that time. I got a lot of material with that little stuffed dinosaur sitting in my lap at banquets and on planes.

  When my son married, I had a *Wedding* category during the six-month buildup to the grand event. You get the idea. Add and drop categories when you have short-term humor ops.

- *Writing up isn't so tough.* I had anticipated that the most difficult task for the group members would be forcing themselves to write up rather than just jot down. Wrong. While they weren't in the habit of turning out vignettes in paragraph form, that did not prove to be difficult once they knew that punctuation and grammar would not be checked.

- *Oh, but finding the time...* All of the participants except one agreed that the most difficult thing was finding the time to write up. They simply didn't have much slack time. For example, they were able to get material every morning when the crowd gathered for morning office chitchat, but when they sat down to go to work, they did just that. They went to work—without writing up.

The one participant who had no problem was a professional speaker who travels often and uses a lot of humor. She used my Jeanne's Journal without change, had lots of slack time, and needed gobs of humorous material, as I do. She produced the greatest results. (The second professional speaker in the group came into the room saying he never wrote anything down. He wanted to hear about the system, but he wasn't changing. And he didn't change.)

The others found, like I found with my in-town journal, that they had to set aside time to fill in the spaces. This meant more jotting down until they could get to that time. For most of them, that was once a day. Be aware before going into the program that you have to plan time to fill in the journal. Then do it.

- *A humor journal is an ongoing process.* One participant who went right by the book was disappointed with her results. She looked and listened and asked, and because she worked at the computer during the day, she chose to write up by hand every night. She thought she would have dozens of great stories. But in several weeks, she had written up only eight really good ones.

The stories were funny, were from her experiences, and were definitely winners, not it'll-do's. Since she gathered them during her work, they would fit beautifully into her presentations. She thought, "But only eight good stories." I thought, "At this pace, she could have over a hundred by the end of the year." It all depends on your perspective. It is important to keep in mind that this is an ongoing, cumulative process.

CLOSING

I have enjoyed sharing my humor philosophy and system for collecting humorous, life-experience speech material. This system has served me well for many years and has actually become my hobby. I don't want to let any funny stuff get away, and my humor journal has been valuable in accomplishing this goal. If you are as serious about life-experience humor as I am, then I strongly suggest that you develop and use some type of humor journal.

A humor journal is not appropriate for every speaker. In sharing my system with all types of speakers, I have received mixed results. Some speakers either didn't have a knack for collecting humor, or thought the process was too time consuming. Others found numerous funny stories during what they considered to be a minimum amount of productive time. You'll have to decide if you want and need an organized system for collecting original stories.

There is one other reason I'm so happy to share my journal system in this book. I finally have an adequate and easy response to the many inquiries that I have had over the years.

To illustrate this, I will close with an answer to the letter in the introduction.

> Dear Aspiring Speaker,
>
> It was great to hear from someone so excited about giving speeches. You asked me where I got my funny, original stories and about my system for collecting humor. I believe your questions are answered in this book, *Don't Let the Funny Stuff Get Away.* It probably contains more than you really wanted to know on the subject, but if you need additional information, please feel free to call.
>
> I wish you well in your pursuit of speaking and in your search for life-experience humor. Above all. . .

Keep 'em laughin'!
Jeanne Robertson

ABOUT THE AUTHOR

Jeanne Robertson, one of America's busiest professional speakers, is known for using hilarious humor from her life experiences. Speaking since 1963, she's been presented every top honor in her profession. In 1989, she was the first woman to be awarded the Cavett, given by the National Speakers Association for long-term contributions to the speaking profession. In 1998, Toastmasters International named her the recipient of its Golden Gavel Award, which is presented annually to an individual who has demonstrated outstanding skills in communication and leadership.

Jeanne won the Miss North Carolina title in 1963 and was named Miss Congeniality in the Miss America Pageant in a vote by the contestants. She is a 1967 graduate of Auburn University, Auburn, Alabama. She taught physical education and coached basketball for nine years before going into professional speaking on a full-time basis.

Jeanne is coauthor of *How the Platform Professionals Keep 'Em Laughin'* and author of *Humor: The Magic of Genie* and *Mayberry Humor Across the USA*.

A Certified Speaking Professional (CSP) and a CPAE Speakers Hall of Fame recipient, Jeanne is a past president of the National Speakers Association, and is a recipient of that organization's Distinguished Service Award. She speaks two languages fluently, English and Southern.

Among her clients and audiences, Jeanne Robertson has a reputation for using funny, original stories. Among her fellow speakers, she is also recognized for urging "Don't let the funny stuff get away."